"Through recollecting threads ([...] ...s or slavery and institutionalized racism in this country, Benders offers theological insights on the relationship between original sin and individual sin as well as the interdependence of liberation."

— Erin Brigham, University of San Francisco

"In *Recollecting America's Original Sin*, Benders invites the reader to travel alongside her in communitas in an admirable quest to 'live justice authentically and inclusively.' It is a personal and deeply moving account of pilgrimage as a powerful means of reckoning as America confronts a long history of racial injustice, as embodied prayer, and—importantly—as a way to begin to heal."

— Kathryn R. Barush, Jesuit School of Theology of Santa Clara University

Recollecting America's Original Sin

A Pilgrimage of Race and Grace

Alison M. Benders

LITURGICAL PRESS
ACADEMIC

Collegeville, Minnesota
www.litpress.org

Cover design by Monica Bokinskie. Painting: *The Fruit Picker* by Dareen Hasan. Used with permission.

Scripture quotations are from the New Revised Standard Version Bible: Anglicised Catholic Edition, copyright © 1989, 1993, 1995 the Division of Christian Education of the National Council of the Churches of Christ in the United States of America. Used by permission. All rights reserved.

1	2	3	4	5	6	7	8	9

Library of Congress Cataloging-in-Publication Data

Names: Benders, Alison M., author.
Title: Recollecting America's original sin : a pilgrimage of race and
    grace / Alison M. Benders.
Description: Collegeville, Minnesota : Liturgical Press Academic,
    [2022] | Includes bibliographical references. | Summary: "Explores
    antiblack racism throughout US history through a Christian
    spirituality lens. The reflections on historical moments and places
    are fashioned as a spiritual pilgrimage that integrates listening,
    reflecting, and daily living"— Provided by publisher.
Identifiers: LCCN 2021051328 (print) | LCCN 2021051329 (ebook) |
    ISBN 9780814665084 (paperback) | ISBN 9780814665336 (epub) |
    ISBN 9780814665336 (pdf)
Subjects: LCSH: Racism—Religious aspects—Christianity. | Race
    relations—Religious aspects—Christianity. | Racism—United
    States. | United States—Race relations. | Christian pilgrims and
    pilgrimages—United States.
Classification: LCC BT734.2 .B46 2022 (print) | LCC BT734.2 (ebook)
    | DDC 277.308/3089—dc23/eng/20211118
LC record available at https://lccn.loc.gov/2021051328
LC ebook record available at https://lccn.loc.gov/2021051329

~ For my brother Drew (1952–2021)—
a pilgrim in spirit and in service

~ For all the members of the
Fall 2018 Race, Justice, and Theology class from JST

~ For my family, with deepest love

Contents

Preface

We live in reckoning times. For years now, daily unprecedented events have challenged reliable routines for Americans. They force on us a reckoning about who we are and what we value. They demand that we declare ourselves for or against. If we remain silent, we are complicit. When we speak, we say too much or not enough. The year 2020 sparked national reckonings long in the making. My pilgrim story visits shrines and holy places in the nation's history to encounter moments that have led to these reckonings. I look through the lens of Black-white racial justice. Our nation's path has also been my own color-line journey as a white woman in an interracial marriage. In walking the color line, I discovered moments of lament, moments of conversion, and gifts of great wisdom.

This race and grace pilgrimage was planned as a Civil Rights journey to be taken in the fall of 2020. A global pandemic interrupted my plans, just as it interrupted the whole world. Since traveling was so limited, and direct human interaction so constrained, this pilgrimage unexpectedly became purer and more intense. I still traveled but, really, from my desk chair, using journals and memories. I filled out my own experiences with the insights of scholars and poets. The pilgrimage lasted longer than I had anticipated even though the circumference of my explorations was reduced to thousands of footsteps, not thousands of miles.

As with all pilgrimages, my color-line path remained a journey seeking transformation. The pandemic, however, stripped away the prospects of travel and spontaneity. The enforced distancing also stripped away distractions. I did not travel far beyond my home community on foot, but the Spirit led me deeply into the desert to reckon with my own sins and the sins of America's white culture.

When I first prepared to take a physical journey to recollect America's original sin, I had anticipated that the actual travel would make up the core of the spiritual encounter. I thought I would move my feet as I prayed myself through our nation's history of slavery, race, and persistent white supremacy. In preparation, I investigated holy sites of resistance and sites saturated with conflict or triumph. I studied our nation's prophets of justice for inspiration and blessing. I considered who might have living water to wash America clean in the struggle to redeem our story on race for this time and place— for a justice-saturated shared future. But COVID disrupted all my calculations. It disrupted the world's expectations. Disruption, I learned, was grace.

In the separate space of a pilgrim time, I recognized our nation's persistent sins as I examined my own conscience. These sins are a failure to love God and the repudiation of God's call to love our neighbors fully and justly. I rambled through U.S. history focusing on the color line dividing Black people and white people, listening for God's appeals, exhortations, and reprimands. I felt myself at a reckoning moment along with our country. I wondered whether we were at a genesis moment, a new creation, when we might begin again on the project of living justly together. I heard God's grace inviting me to convert my heart and dwell in a covenant community—a beloved community where all belong.

My pilgrim path to recollect America's original sin, therefore, led me deeply into pivotal moments of our nation's history. I pieced them together during the world's pandemic pause. Some historic moments were jumping-off points for faith connections. Other moments connected with places in Louisiana, Alabama, and Georgia that I had visited as a part of a class, Civil Rights Immersion, during the fall of 2018. Still others came from personal experience, either places and events from my family's story or places in my city that I was able to visit during the spring of 2021. Like landmarks upon a pilgrim's path, the moments strung together from history, memory, and imagination became a real journey recollecting America's original sin. The selected moments, few among so many possible, ignited my desire to respond faithfully to the reckonings of our time that have called us to justice.

I thank God for graces rained upon me along this pilgrim path—for the time apart, for wise guides with discerning words, for the cloud of witnesses who accompanied me, for the unexpected hope that justice is possible in a kairos moment.

I invite others to join me in this sacred pilgrimage space. No preparation is necessary; all that's needed is an open heart ready to encounter what may come. This book is not a travel guide or a theological treatise. We're on a pilgrimage. Accept each separate moment as an invitation to savor the place or situation with grace and possibility. We can become *communitas*, a community bound into a shared hope by walking and praying together. According to the ancient Israelite prayer: *Shema!* Hear, O Israel! Love God and love your neighbor with your whole being!

For me, *Shema!* has been the Spirit's summons to walk with wide-open eyes and then respond. Walk with me! *Shema!*

Alison M. Benders
Berkeley, California / Cleveland Heights, Ohio
Pentecost Sunday 2021

First Week
On the Threshold of a Journey

Journey in the major Western religious traditions signifies a courageous risk undertaken to dwell according to God's promised blessings. Journeys are future facing. A pilgrim's journey has a sacred goal, like the promised-land journey woven into our country's founding stories. The idea of a holy journey shimmers as our national root paradigm because we use it to explain ourselves.[1] Closely related to journey in the American ethos is freedom, another root paradigm. Freedom represents the culminating, intangible blessing that God dispenses to the faithful. Journey and freedom consecrate our national identity. Almost reflexively, these ideologies frame who we are and what we are about.

Moment 1: Reckoning

I started this pilgrimage in the run-up to Election Day 2020 in the United States, a rather portentous day to journey along the country's color line. Our national conversations for months had radiated danger, like a tinderbox ready to burst into fire. They reminded me of the charged atmosphere in the Berkeley Hills during the fall drought time, when the tiniest spark may ignite racing, windblown flames. Our national veneer of democracy, which veils split and splintered communities, seemed

---

[1] Victor Turner, *Dramas, Fields, and Metaphors: Symbolic Action in Human Society* (Ithaca, NY: Cornell University Press, 1974), 67.

1

poised to combust in the withering public peace before the election. The opening verse of Psalm 63 reverberated through my waking hours: we live "as in a dry and weary land where there is no water."[2] My pilgrim hope was that our struggles would yield a quenching rain, like the thunderstorm along a powerful front that leaves a new peace in its wake. I hoped that God might give us living water to refresh and recreate our community life.

Unexpectedly, during this pilgrimage into America's original sin, I experienced grace within our shameful history of racial oppression. The lens of deep human community became a touchstone for me on this journey. A covenanted community where all people belong has been the heart of America's most life-giving identity, though it has often been strained and incompletely lived. A fiercely urgent demand confronts our nation in these days, a demand to live justice authentically and inclusively.

America's racial reckoning is an intertwined reckoning. Racial oppression intersects with other long-standing injustices of gender, climate, ethnicity, wealth, and health. How did our nation get here? Is there a just way forward for us? Where will we find healing waters? Since I wanted to understand how we might live more justly, I needed to go "on pilgrimage." These unsettling questions drove me into a separate space where I could confront the meaning of the deep and tragic color line that has divided people in this country.

It seems that pilgrimages are all the rage these days. So many different retreats from daily life are claimed as pilgrimages, although most bear only a remote resemblance to the ancient spiritual quests for transformation. Transformation is the hallmark of a pilgrimage. Pilgrimages are journeys "undertaken in the light of a story. A great event has happened. . . . The

---

[2] For translations from Scripture, see *Holy Bible: Catholic Edition, Anglicized Text, NRSV, New Revised Standard Version*, illustrated by Kathleen Edwards (New York: Harper Catholic Bibles, 2007).

pilgrim seeks not only to confirm the experience of others firsthand but to be changed by the experience."[3] Pilgrimages are more than hikes or history tours. They cannot be relaxing jaunts to folk shrines to drink from the holy grail or kiss the Blarney stone. Pilgrimages represent a radical spiritual discipline, a pathway apart from daily life. Since ancient times, human beings have ventured on holy paths pursuing wisdom and transformation. Quest, encounter, and transformation intersect with the pilgrims' own experiences. Animating every step is the pilgrims' openness to be changed, their readiness for regeneration.

As pilgrims depart from daily life, they enter liminal space. "Liminal" is a strange but useful word to signify an edgy place beyond routine boundaries. Liminal space and time are neither here nor there. Pilgrims place themselves neither here nor there in order to become new. Only when we take a full-stop pause in our lives can we venture vulnerably into the past and the present and possibly walk into a transformed future. Although I remained COVID-isolated in Cleveland Heights, Ohio, through my period of study, reflection, and prayer, I used the symbolism of a four-week journey to pace and pray. With seven moments in each week, I crossed a pilgrim's threshold into a wilderness of history and hope, entrusting myself to God's care.

On pilgrimage, time is paused but full of possibilities—a pregnant pause. Greek offers us the evocative word *kairos* to signify time set apart. Entering kairos time means being fully present in the sacred moment of now. In a related way, the now-ness of kairos signifies the appropriate time for action. Now is the time! These four weeks were *now* moments when I could dig deeply into the meaning of race in the United States. Mirroring our nation's racial history, my kairos journey was not strictly linear or chronological. In the blessed wayfaring

[3] Paul Elie, *The Life You Save May Be Your Own: An American Pilgrimage* (New York: Macmillan Press, 2004), x.

months away from ordinary work, time and events converged to saturate my thoughts and prayers, my readings and conversations. The saturation enabled me to link together the past and present layers of America's painful, shameful, stumbling justice journey.

Henry David Thoreau's musings on walking as sauntering also described my experience on pilgrimage.[4] Colloquially, "to saunter" means to traipse or stroll along. But "saunter," Thoreau contended, encapsulates two complementary ideas from its French roots. First, it means *sans terre*, "without land or a home location." A foreigner or homeless person is *sans terre*. Thoreau, however, preferred the derivation of "saunter" from the French phrase *sainte terre*, meaning "holy land." He christened pilgrims and walkers as "holy landers" because they journeyed along sacred paths. A pilgrim saunterer is one who leaves home to encounter the divine in a holy wasteland or sacred set-apart time. The word "peregrination" sports a similar ambiguous signification. *Peregrinus* in Latin means "foreigner" or "stranger," like a peregrine falcon. During much of my kairos time, I felt like an itinerant roamer, a stranger, or (as walkers along the Way of St. James are dubbed) a *peregrina*.

Nevertheless, a pilgrimage is not simply peregrination and aimless sauntering. The pilgrim's quest, regardless of the specific question, strives to engage what is holy because of its deeper meaning. The quest itself, its when-where-and-how itinerary, depends on the traveler's context. The seeker's life situation dictates the general direction, while the events of the pilgrim's past frame the essential questions. That was certainly true of this race and grace pilgrimage for me. This kairos journey started as a reckoning and ended with deepened convictions and a commitment to respond. A conversion. The journey wasn't a straight high road but a path in the wilderness. I created the path as I walked it. I followed faint tracks and

---

[4] Henry Thoreau, "Walking," *Atlantic Monthly* (June 1862), reprinted *Atlantic Monthly* (October 2020).

bypasses; I hit dead ends, and I made side trips to explore our nation's past and my own. Walk with me.

Moment 2: "When You Pray, Move Your Feet"

The words of the great freedom fighter John Lewis, who died in the summer of 2020, spoke directly to me on this pilgrimage. During the Civil Rights marches of the 1960s, he inspired protesters with the African proverb "When you pray, move your feet."[5] Pilgrimage is prayer in motion. Praying and moving go hand in hand for seekers, for protesters, and for pilgrims.

The color-line expedition described in this book was not my first pilgrimage. I had previously accompanied students and colleagues from the Jesuit School of Theology to Spain, to follow in the footsteps of St. Ignatius, and to the American South, to witness monuments of the Civil Rights Movement.[6] Walking the color line, however, was my first solo pilgrimage. Set apart by myself, I wanted to bring the questions that were weighing heavily on my own heart to God for wisdom and healing. More

[5] John Lewis, interview by Krista Tippett, "Love in Action," *The On Being Project*, NPR, July 28, 2020, https://onbeing.org/programs/john-lewis-love-in-action.

[6] I journeyed on a Civil Rights pilgrimage in the fall of 2018 with the Jesuit School of Theology class called Race, Justice, and Theology. Our odyssey formed the foundation of some moments that I recollect during the second and third weeks in this account. A priest from the Diocese of Orange, CA, co-taught this course with me. I am sincerely grateful for the weeklong pilgrimage that he had planned for us using his network of justice communities in New Orleans and Alabama. The students who shared their faith and hearts on the Civil Rights pilgrimage included Sandra Dratler, Jeff Dorr, Joshua Peters, Zach Presutti, Ellen Jewett, Janet Katari, Maika Heffelfinger, and Calvin Nixon. We used the term "holy remembrance," which I first heard from one of the students, as a touchstone for the troubling, challenging, but God-present moments that we experienced. I use the first person in this book to aid the meditative flow of my recollections, but the students were beside me for many of the moments. I am eternally grateful for their witness, and I have dedicated *Recollecting America's Original Sin* to them.

than that, I wanted to walk in the freedom fighters' footsteps, hoping that their courage would embrace and embolden me.

Psalm 51: Prayer of Repentance

[1] "Have mercy on me, O God,
    according to your steadfast love;
according to your abundant mercy
    blot out my transgressions.
[2] Wash me thoroughly from my iniquity,
    and cleanse me from my sin.

[3] "For I know my transgressions,
    and my sin is ever before me.
[4] Against you, you alone, have I sinned,
    and done what is evil in your sight,
so that you are justified in your sentence
    and blameless when you pass judgement.
[5] Indeed, I was born guilty,
    a sinner when my mother conceived me.

[6] "You desire truth in the inward being;
    therefore teach me wisdom in my secret heart.
[7] Purge me with hyssop, and I shall be clean;
    wash me, and I shall be whiter than snow.
[8] Let me hear joy and gladness;
    let the bones that you have crushed rejoice.
[9] Hide your face from my sins,
    and blot out all my iniquities.

[10] "Create in me a clean heart, O God,
    and put a new and right spirit within me.
[11] Do not cast me away from your presence,
    and do not take your holy spirit from me.
[12] Restore to me the joy of your salvation,
    and sustain in me a willing spirit.

[13] "Then I will teach transgressors your ways,
    and sinners will return to you.

¹⁴ Deliver me from bloodshed, O God,
    O God of my salvation,
and my tongue will sing aloud of your deliverance.

¹⁵ "O Lord, open my lips,
    and my mouth will declare your praise.
¹⁶ For you have no delight in sacrifice;
    if I were to give a burnt offering, you would not be
    pleased.
¹⁷ The sacrifice acceptable to God is a broken spirit;
    a broken and contrite heart, O God, you will not despise.

¹⁸ "Do good to Zion in your good pleasure;
    rebuild the walls of Jerusalem,
¹⁹ then you will delight in right sacrifices,
    in burnt offerings and whole burnt offerings;
    then bulls will be offered on your altar."

As I paced on pilgrimage these past months, I had three holy
supports. First, Psalm 51 spoke out my repentance. Its ancient
penitential cadences had long been an anchor for me in turbulent times. Catholics who pray the Liturgy of the Hours know
at least verse 15 of the *Miserere* by heart: "O Lord, open my lips,
/ and my mouth will declare your praise." But there is a more
powerful theme in this great hymn—repentance seeking hope.
"Have mercy on me, O God, / according to your steadfast love;
/ according to your abundant mercy / blot out my transgressions" (v. 1). Praying these opening words settled me on this
pilgrimage. On my best days, I dropped my guard and came
clean about my shortcomings. I often jumped to the kernel of
contrition in the psalm, sincerely seeking a new vision—God's
vision for the world: "You desire truth in the inward being; /
therefore teach me wisdom in my secret heart" (v. 6). The final
verse assured me of God's covenantal faithfulness. It promised
that God's people would be able to offer "right sacrifices,"

which grace would amplify (v. 19). The prayer of Catholic repentance provided me a community to belong to, a pilgrim's *communitas*. I felt embraced by like-souled trekkers during this desk-chair *camino*, knowing that people around the world were also praying the sacred penitential words of the *Miserere*. Together with a cloud of witnesses, I prayed for God's mercy, God's forgiveness, and the wisdom of the Holy Spirit.

The second support, more tactile, was my father's shillelagh that I claimed as my own by decorating it with multicolored ribbons. A shillelagh is an Irish walking stick. Actually, it's more of a pummeling, trouncing kind of battle stick, not a simple cane to steady stumbling legs. The shillelagh was polished smooth by the hands of my unseen ancestors who had clutched it for support and safety. The staff enfleshed for me a dim, collective memory of terror, when my forebears four generations ago fled the potato famine, a genocide at the hands of the British government to arrive in the New York harbor. Our family stories flowed into the streams of migrant trauma in U.S. history: captives shackled in shadowy ship holds, ragged walkers carting overstuffed immigrant satchels, and proud Native peoples who had lived on the land and then died of white sicknesses as well as by violence at the hands of white settlers. This pilgrimage laid bare for me the unhealed traumas that to this day continue to fester.

The blackthorn shillelagh with its knobby handle remained propped against my study wall throughout my journey. Above it hung a framed print, small and simple, which was my third support. The print's elegant calligraphy glimmered against a background shading from purple to rose. It illuminated Mark 12:29-31, when a scribe asked Jesus which commandment was first, that is, the greatest.

> Jesus answered, "The first is, 'Hear, O Israel: the Lord our God, the Lord is one; you shall love the Lord your God with all your heart, and with all your soul, and with all your mind, and with all your strength.' The second is this,

'You shall love your neighbor as yourself.' There is no other commandment greater than these."[7]

The sound of *Shema!* drew me in so that I studied its meaning. The Shema is the first prayer Jewish newborns hear whispered in their ears at birth and is the last words for the dying. It declares the oneness of God and the community in their mutual allegiance sealed by the Torah covenant. The Israelites received the Ten Commandments with this awareness: "If we diligently observe this entire commandment before the LORD our God, as [God] has commanded us, we will be in the right" (Deut 6:25).[8] Moses assured the people of God's reciprocal care: "If you heed these ordinances . . . , [God] will love you, bless you, and multiply you. . . . You shall be the most blessed of peoples" (Deut 7:12-14). On this pilgrimage, *Shema!* meant for me the command to tune into God: "Listen! Pay attention!"

Then I realized that *Shema!* meant more. In the relationship between God and the Israelites, *Shema!* meant not only to listen but, more potently, to respond. To call out "Listen!" also demands that the covenant partners respond to what they hear because of the binding relationship. The people demanded care from God precisely because of God's promised fidelity back to them. For example, Psalm 27:7 reads, "Hear, O LORD, when I cry aloud, / be gracious to me and answer me!" Confident in the people's covenant with God, the psalmist cried out "*Shema!*" to God. The Exodus story demonstrated the same mutual trust. The Israelites' groans for deliverance rose up to Yahweh. *Shema!* demanded God's attention and God's swift

---

[7] The translation in the illumination is from the New Revised Standard Version Bible: Catholic Edition © 1989, 1993. The illumination can be viewed at "Explore *The Saint John's Bible*," The Saint John's Bible, https://saintjohns bible.org/See/Explore_Book#book/861.

[8] The same exchange is recorded in the book of Exodus, as the Israelites committed themselves to God: "All that the LORD has spoken we will do, and we will be obedient" (24:7).

response because the psalmist knew that the people dwelled together with God. Therefore, they could expect God to respond.

I then connected *Shema!* to the Christian gospel. Jesus often punctuated parables with the admonishment "Let those who have eyes, see! Let those who have ears, hear!" A *Shema!* interpretation might be "Let those who have eyes and ears pay attention and respond."

Shema! for me came to mean first that I must proclaim allegiance to God, the one God. It also meant that I had to lean into God's vision for a beloved community. *Shema!* included the injunction to act justly. Psalm 51 and *Shema!* became my pilgrim prayers. Leaning on the shillelagh and whispering "*Shema!*" centered my attention on the signs and stories around me. Praying for heart-wisdom reminded me to listen to what God's Spirit would reveal on this journey from past to present. The prayers reminded me to love God as fully as I could—not an abstraction of God, but God fully present in each person and place I encountered. In the silence of my heart, I heard "*Shema!*" I heard God calling me to a reckoning in a whisper both ancient and ever new: "*Shema!* Listen! Pay attention! Do something!"

As I moved my feet, I prayed for the Spirit to open my eyes and ears so that I might respond to what I encountered.

Moment 3: Mr. Jefferson's Shadow

To fulfill the imperative of paying attention, I started my color-line pilgrimage in Charlottesville, Virginia, my childhood home. Recollecting Charlottesville led me directly into the shade of Thomas Jefferson's radical impact on this country's identity. "Radical" connotes both renegade and foundational, as Jefferson's writings were in the formation of the country. His idealistic pragmatism palpably permeated the life and landscape of the still-small city of Charlottesville, which is home to the university he founded. Jefferson's political influence straddled our country's transition from a collection of colonies to a union of states. The generously proportioned, neoclassical buildings parading along the stately downtown pedestrian mall and along the bustling University Corner displayed his eloquent synthesis of past and possibility. They enfleshed Jefferson's ideals for our experimental republic. Clear, white-framed windows piercing rose brick walls symbolized how past endeavors of human community could be perfected through the wisdom of enlightened progress. It's no coincidence that even today the University of Virginia's famed Rotunda grants Charlottesville's residents a direct line of sight to the iconic dome of Monticello just three miles south, perched on the side of Carter Mountain in the Appalachian Piedmont.

At the University of Virginia, people traditionally introduced the founder not as President Jefferson or Thomas Jefferson but, with southern regard, as *Mr. Jefferson*. Because my father taught in Clark Hall at the Law School in the 1960s, we children felt embraced within the general reverence for Mr. Jefferson's university ideals. His imposing shadow and Monticello's ever-present gaze remained mythic in our childhood memories. During my earliest years, our family lived first in graduate student housing on campus and later in a new neighborhood of ranch houses, mimosa trees, and school bus stops. We played on the Lawn behind the Rotunda during festivals. From time to time, we visited with the families of distinguished professors, who were privileged to live in the anachronistic residences that lined the Lawn with lush gardens behind the serpentine walls. We treasured Mr. Jefferson as our familiar, certainly a hero, maybe even kin. I was too young to notice whether the university troubled itself with Jefferson's infidelity to his freedom ideals. As kids, we celebrated his Declaration of Independence and recited his assertion that equality was an inalienable human right. Still, I felt that our family dwelled apart from Charlottesville and the university because I sensed that our family values were out of step with the Southern culture of Virginia.

Charlottesville and the state of Virginia had long been epi-
centers of racial strife but had also made strides toward racial
justice. Slivers of memory remain with me. Black families lived
on the south side of the town, in the "old Scottsville" neighborhood on the way to Monticello, the wrong side of town across
the railroad tracks. White families lived north of the 250
Bypass, in the new neighborhoods along Route 29 North to
Washington. In the years after *Brown v. Board of Education*, with
federal desegregation mandates for restaurants and other public accommodations, some white residents of Charlottesville
were aghast that Black diners might eat at the town's famous
Buddy's Restaurant. I recalled gawking in wide-eyed wonder
at Buddy's whitewashed walls and shuttered windows as my
father drove us past. According to our family ethos, such owners were "prejudiced," individuals who refused to give Black
people their due. Lane High School, all white since it was built,
was closed for a couple of years in the 1960s. A heated court
battle finally resulted in Charlottesville constructing a new
campus to educate all high school students in the city. In these
same years, Mr. Jefferson's university began haltingly integrating its own student body, starting with the Law School, where
my father was an impressionable student and then a fledgling
professor.[9]

While on this color-line pilgrimage, I read many volumes of
my father's mid-twentieth-century library on "race relations."
Serendipitously, I found Robert Penn Warren's 1956 report
Segregation: The Inner Conflict in the South.[10] The Black and white
voices that Penn Warren quoted jumped off the page as I read
them. I could hear the Appalachian accent and the Virginia

---

[9] For a timeline of 1950s to 1970s events contextualizing the University of
Virginia's integration within larger national events, see "An Epoch of Change:
A Timeline of the University 1955–1975," in the series *Trailblazing Against
Tradition*, accessed February 2, 2021, http://www2.vcdh.virginia.edu/lawn
/HarrisonI/Timeline.html.

[10] Robert Penn Warren, *Segregation: The Inner Conflict in the South* (New
York: Vintage Books, 1956).

aristocratic drawl behind the words. I felt the triggering threats of violence against "Negroes," threats that were tenuously held in check by thin social conventions. I heard segregation praised quite unapologetically. White people asserted: "Segregation is the law of God, not man. . . . Continue to rob the white race in order to bribe the Asiatic and Negro and these people will overwhelm the white race and destroy all progress, religion, invention, art and return us to the jungle."[11] One speaker, identifying himself as a redneck, said: "They [rednecks] will feel the rub. He is the one on the underside of the plane with nothing between him and bare black ground. He's got to have something to give him pride. Just to be better than something."[12] A white woman summarized: "But of course we have to keep the white race intact"; her husband corrected: "In power—in power—you mean the white race in power."[13] White supremacy in thought, word, and deed was clearly on display; it was simply a matter of fact in the 1950s.

Even as I read these words, protected by sixty years and five hundred miles, my gut squirmed, anticipating danger. I had a potent word now to name the evil they perceived— miscegenation, racial mixing. Black men knowing white women was the particularly abhorrent crime for which the white community threatened the most vicious sanction: lynching. A half century on, I recognized that the conflicts reshaping America, between Jim Crow and Civil Rights, all swirled together in the tiny crucible of Charlottesville, Virginia.

In the summer of 2017, Charlottesville came again to national and international attention as a battleground over white domination. White neoconservatives swamped the city on August 11 and 12, marching from the Rotunda to the cobblestoned downtown mall with torches and vile taunts to "Unite the right." Counterprotester Heather Heyer lost her life resisting

---

[11] Penn Warren, *Segregation*, 43.
[12] Penn Warren, 43–44.
[13] Penn Warren, 44.

white supremacy, mowed down by another white citizen enraged at those who defended racial equality. The rally seemed
incongruous with Charlottesville's customarily staid streets.
It posed perennial questions to America: Whose nation is this?
Who belongs? I wondered whether Mr. Jefferson's ideals really
meant that *all* people were equal. Like the nation he shaped,
Jefferson walked a calamitous color line, a cursed, never-
resolved moral paradox between freedom and enslavement.

> "We hold these truths to be self-evident, that all men are
> created equal, that they are endowed by their Creator with
> certain unalienable Rights, that among these are Life, Liberty
> and the pursuit of Happiness.—That to secure these rights,
> Governments are instituted among Men, deriving their just
> powers from the consent of the governed."
>
> United States Declaration of Independence, 1776

We certainly knew as children that, on the mountaintop
overlooking his grand educational experiment, Jefferson held
in bondage his own children as well as a whole village. A half
century ago, tours of the early presidents' homes, such as President George Washington's plantation estate of Mount Vernon,
showcased graciously repaired grounds and meticulously refurbished chambers that had swathed white owners in ele-
gance and luxury. Guidebooks of the era scarcely hinted at the
men, women, and children who had been imprisoned in dirt-
floored cabins, the individuals whose forced labor had produced the unparalleled comfort for their enslavers. In recent
years, Monticello tours have foregrounded Jefferson's moral
struggles alongside his genius for political leadership and
technological innovation. Just as much as his mixed-race prog-
eny, Jefferson was sin-bound by Virginia's slaveholding stric-
tures. Our ingenious white patriarch and founder did not,
would not—and perhaps could not—emancipate the people
he enslaved during his lifetime.

As I examined my childhood Charlottesville roots, I wondered at the country's fitful progress to eliminate the racial injustice that is baked into our interpersonal relationships, into our myths, and into our laws and policies. Few white people realize that historians can pinpoint when notions of racial caste developed, yielding the first laws that permanently enslaved Africans and their descendants. [14] It was the Virginia assembly in the seventeenth century. European indentured servants were also categorized then as enslaved labor, except that their oppression had a limit. Ibram Kendi notes that, once Black people were consigned to slavery, whites demonized and belittled them. European colonists throughout the Americas created the laws and systems to lock Africans into their subordinated status mainly because it was lucrative to do so. Settlers and enslavers of European ancestry accepted this situation because they firmly believed in a hierarchy of human races based on color. The white "race" placed itself at the peak of human progress and identified itself as God's most favored people. White colonists placed darker-skinned people at the bottom rung of human value; their dark skin and "uncivilized" behavior were evidence of God's own judgment about their worth. Other non-whites were caught in the same trap, controlled by the same interlocking ideologies of economic and social exploitation.

I tried to put myself in Jefferson's mind. He was well aware that Virginia's laws profoundly belied his thrilling words that all people were equal. Jefferson's biographer Annette Gordon-Reed's assessment offers nuance but does not morally exonerate him in my mind. Jefferson as patriarch at Monticello controlled the lives of all his dependents, free and enslaved.

---

[14] There is substantial research to support this brief account. See, e.g., Christina Proenza-Coles, *American Founders: How People of African Descent Established Freedom in the New World* (Montgomery, AL: NewSouth Books, 2019); and Ibram Kendi, *Stamped from the Beginning: The Definitive History of Racist Ideas in America* (New York: Hachette UK, 2016).

In the eighteenth-century culture that formed him, "[s]lavery was not just an economic system. It was a system of social control."[15] He felt that the order of society had to be preserved against the chaos of humanity's more vicious impulses. Social order was paramount. Gordon-Reed explained Jefferson's priorities:

> [H]e felt that he helped to found a country. . . . Breaking with Great Britain, setting up a government, that was a pretty big deal, and that the next generation of people had something to do, as well, and that was to make the progress on the issue of slavery that he thought could be made. . . . The American Revolution was the most important thing in his life. And the tragedy is he couldn't see that, after the union is formed, that the thing that would split it apart would be the institution of slavery. . . . [H]e definitely thought that mankind and society would get better and better.[16]

My ephemeral Charlottesville memories have now been fleshed out with adult sensibilities and validated with more understanding. Deep chagrin nevertheless weighted my heart when I realized that our white-dominated nation would make the same compromises nearly 250 years after Jefferson had swapped Black liberty for white wealth. He left the battle over the emancipation of Africans and their descendants to his successors. His belief in a progressively rosier future obscured his capacity to assess the full cost of the Faustian bargain he had made. From America's founding, the terms of our sin were set. *Shema!*

---

[15] Annette Gordon-Reed, interview by Shankar Vedantam, "A Founding Contradiction: Thomas Jefferson's Stance on Slavery," *NPR: Hidden Brain*, November 26, 2018, www.npr.org/2018/11/26/670803601/a-founding -contradiction-thomas-jeffersons-stance-on-slavery.

[16] Gordon-Reed, "Founding Contradiction."

Moment 4: Teach Your Children Well

This self-guided, grace-guided pilgrimage demanded a further excavation of my formative years, my own founding, so to speak. Traveling into the past revealed the color line that I had walked for much of my life. The fortunate position I enjoyed as the daughter of a law professor at Mr. Jefferson's University of Virginia colored my grasp of racism, so to speak, in ways that took me years to realize.

My parents became adults in post–*Brown v. Board of Education* Charlottesville, during the Second Vatican Council and the church-shuddering years that followed. In the heady, roiling days of the early '60s, my parents regularly welcomed one new baby after another into our compact starter home until we were stacked to the rafters in bunk beds and basement bedrooms. As idealistic young parents, the Civil Rights protests vividly displayed on the nightly news had deeply inflected their political and social development during these impressionable years.

Like many Catholics born in the Depression era, my parents' religious affinity dictated their communal and personal identities. Bound by Catholic expectations, they dutifully joined Holy Comforter Church in Charlottesville during their law student years. Because the town was growing, the parish established an extension community to support new families at Branchlands, just beyond the city limits. Our lives revolved around the square stone chapel at the far side of the bus parking lot, kitty-corner from the Dominican convent. The school building consisted of nine classrooms along the main hallway, one for each grade, K–8. Every grade boasted twenty-five or more students taught by a stern-faced nun in a floor-length black-and-white habit, rosary beads at her waist. A few offices and the lunchroom completed the building's floor plan. School families religiously attended Mass every Sunday and then processed to the cafeteria to celebrate holy days according to the colorful Catholic year: purple for Advent and Lent, red for Holy Week, white for the Easter season, and green for Ordinary

Time. We relished smoky incense at High Masses and splashes of holy water for baptisms and blessings. We exalted in gritty smudges on our foreheads for Ash Wednesday and cheered for the Three Kings cake at Epiphany on the twelfth day of Christmas. We collected holy cards for good deeds and traded them along with our bundles of baseball cards and bags of marbles. Catholics weren't very common in Charlottesville, but this was our world, and we stuck together.

A visit to Branchlands years later showed me just how tiny that world was. Convinced that a white-bearded God beamed down graciously on our playground lines of boys and girls, I learned my doctrine through morning hymns. We sang our allegiance to God and country in the shivering moments before a shrill bell called us to lessons. When my classmates and I started third grade, taught for decades by Mrs. Cox in Room 4, something unprecedented happened: as dark-skinned Philip joined our class, we transitioned with little fanfare to an integrated world. I don't recall that we welcomed him, but I don't recall that we spurned him. I never asked what it cost him or how he felt. Images of Philip's eager innocence have remained with me. He would send silly love couplets to fair-haired girls despite the racial strife on our doorstep. In many southern hamlets of the day, such childish crushes brought storms of disaster upon Black boys. In our little school, I just barely sensed unmentionable fears of desperate, hate-fed violence threatening from the shadows, so I never said a word about the notes. Philip's presence in third grade taught me more practically about white and Black in the segregated South than our father's abstract lessons ever could.

Still, school memories for me intersected with a thin but admiring understanding of my father's academic work. I vaguely understood that he taught "civil rights," which in those days encompassed school desegregation in the South, but I was not quite sure what else. At dinner, he would expound upon the principles of equality for his growing family. Our limited grasp of the "signs of the times" conferred a hero's aura on him, and the ugliness of white resistance remained condemned through unspoken judgments. In my imagination, he rode astride the proverbial white horse of justice. Although I didn't really know much about academic life, I believed his was a valiant, countercultural career on the right side of history.

Later, in the 1970s, our family moved from Charlottesville to chase my father's professional aspirations. My parents weren't activists, per se, but their witness to racial justice still involved the whole family. Without flourish or fuss, their choices embodied the church's mission in the world. They settled us in neighborhoods in the inner-ring suburbs of Midwestern cities because these border towns were trying to integrate their schools and neighborhoods. We attended public schools in Evanston on the edge of Chicago, taking city buses to downtown YMCA clubs where we practiced self-governance and community service. In North Avondale in Cincinnati, we lived as token Christians welcomed by a close community of Holocaust survivors, finding best friends among the daughters and sons of Jewish doctors and lawyers, and we lived with other white families resisting white flight. Finally, we landed in Shaker Heights on the border of Cleveland, a suburb famed for its carefully crafted visionary path to integration through excellent public services and schools. My mother joined the workforce through politics, which provided a direct way for her to build up the community and engage the struggle for racial justice on her terms. Her only full-time job was eight years as Shaker Heights's first woman mayor. She located the Around the World Playground, excellent new ball fields, and the Shaker Family Center in city neighborhoods where the economic need was greatest and, predictably, where many Black families lived. Her no-nonsense leadership assured that taxpayers' dollars supported those families who needed community resources the most to build for themselves a middle-class life.

Thomas Jefferson banked on human progress as steady, as a long arc bending irreversibly toward justice. Unfortunately, our nation's journey has been a pendulum of progress and regress. Our individual and shared steps have been halting and incomplete. But I have learned something about the importance of striving even for precarious progress. My parents so vividly fired their children's imaginations with the notion of justice that five of their nine children, including myself, became lawyers. Most of their children have also become scholars, coaches, and teachers, myself included. All of us have been faithful to the struggle for racial justice in our personal and professional lives. As in Jesus' parables of planting and harvest, seeds planted in good ground and well-tended will yield a rich harvest. Teach your children well!

But despite formation as bold as our parents gave us, my too-hopeful naivete confronted me as I paced through these pilgrimage moments. Our country cannot simply walk away from the fetters of enslavement and segregation and expect them to vanish. The 1960s laws that eliminated the color-line barriers and asserted legal equality were (again) incomplete. Nearly sixty years on from the triumphs of the Voting Rights Act and the Civil Rights Act, every day the struggle to build a just, inclusive community still demands our faithful actions because we have not arrived yet. Justice will not arise unless we choose it. More radical than realizing that racism was embedded in American institutions, I came to know that America's original sin is also enfleshed within us.

Moment 5: Ties That Bind

Communitas is a complex word in a pilgrim's vocabulary and experience. It refers to the shared sacred community that quickly develops with fellow wayfarers on any pilgrimage. We become human beings by walking with others along the pilgrimage of life. We become united by sharing experiences of adversity and triumph. We find power and meaning when we are tied to others through past struggles. At the same time, we cannot let the past harden into constricting fetters that bind us. On this race and grace pilgrimage, I discovered so much about the ties that bind this country.

Howard Thurman gazed out over the ocean one night as he journeyed toward Europe. The sobering thoughts of captive Africans who had crossed over a similar watery wilderness gripped his heart. He mused:

> From my cabin window I look out on the full moon and the ghosts of my forefathers rise and fall with the undulating waves. Across these same waters how many years ago they came! What were the inchoate mutterings locked tight within the circle of their hearts? In the deep, heavy darkness of the foul-smelling hold of the ship, where they could not see the sky, nor hear the night noises, nor feel the warm compassion of the tribe, they held their breath against the agony. . . . How does the human spirit accommodate itself to desolation? How did they? What tools of the spirit were in their hands with which to cut a path through the wilderness of their despair?[17]

Thurman recollected in his imagination the bewildering anguish of his African ancestors who had been kidnapped centuries ago across the vast Atlantic Ocean. He was a descendant of women and men shackled in ships' holds against their wills. Thurman's reflection on the Atlantic crossing conjured up an infinite agony of being locked up, assaulted by the nauseating smells and terrorized moans of other captive human beings. His questions fathomed the depths of personal extinction that his own ancestors faced. Still, he wondered whether, even in their dehumanized captivity, they possessed the "tools of the spirit" that might "cut a path through the wilderness of their despair."

I noticed how, in retelling his ancestors' captive journey across the ocean, Thurman bound himself to America's founding

[17] Howard Thurman, *Deep River and the Negro Spiritual Speaks of Life and Death* (Richmond, IN: Howard Thurman Books, 1975), 5.

story. Exodus—the story of God rescuing the Israelites from slavery by leading them through the wilderness—is one strand of our precious national identity. Exodus speaks of slavery and freedom, tyranny and emancipation. Exodus is another root religious paradigm that unites people in this country even though we have deeply conflicting interpretations of what it means and how to claim it. Exodus has been our national religion, it seems.

Exodus continues to shape American imaginations even though fewer and fewer people practice religion religiously. Religious, *re-ligio*. The Latin origins of the word "religion" reveal its meaning. The prefix *re-* means *again*, as in many English words like "redo," "reorganize," or "reimagine." The remainder of the word derives from *ligare*, to tie or bind as a ligature does. So true. Religions connect us over and over again with humankind's unquenchable thirst for the divine. Religions link human beings with life-giving expressions of larger, cosmic meaning. Founding national stories like Exodus express who we are and why we are, but as I learned on this color-line pilgrimage, Exodus has many meanings, as complex and nuanced as the colors of our neighbors' bodies.

The Exodus juxtaposition of tyranny and freedom beat in rhythm with my pilgrim steps. Our daily language offered a glimpse into what matters in our culture. Here I thought of common American idioms like "ties that bind" or "bound away." Enslaved Africans—literally captured and bound—were shackled and forced to this land. Theirs was not deliverance to the promised land of Canaan where they could expect milk and honey. Their unloading on these shores was more akin to the subjugated Israelites' exile in Egypt. Negro spirituals voiced the Black existential hope that they would be "free at last," a hope reverberating over centuries and resisting dehumanization in every new form of enslavement that white culture devised. In contrast, Europeans sailing to this continent framed their story as a heroic freedom-asserting journey. They saw themselves as bound away to a new land where they would be

free. The treacherous seventeenth-century transatlantic crossing for the religious protestants, literally the people who protested, signaled emancipation from monarchy and tyranny.
Protestants journeying to America were convinced that God
was leading them, like the Israelites, to a promised land. They
read God's favor and affirmation into their heroic adventures
and desperate struggles for life and liberty. With every over-
crested wave, they shed the fetters of past sufferings by framing
themselves as a chosen people, God's elect. Native Americans,
indigenous to this land, have also been bound away in a per-
verted inversion of Exodus. The nineteenth-century Trail of
Tears forced tribes from their homelands into reservations,
desert wildernesses of bondage and extermination, certainly
not a promised land.

"Bound and determined" also celebrates another mythic
American trait. It means that nothing will stop Americans. We
are intrepid. We are people who get things done, we are cap-
tains of our own fate, and we make the world conform to our
demands. This expression is tinged with feelings of inevitability. We predict events that are bound to happen. "There's
bound to be rain on our school picnic," we glumly anticipate.
Or, of our particularly successful and determined friends, we
say: "They're bound to be millionaires!" These phrases communicate an underlying sense of inevitability or obligation.
Certainty and clear outcomes go hand in glove with being
events bound to happen.

"Bound" also signals constraint for those on the margins or
those still on the way to emancipation. Boundaries are limits.
Fences mark the dividing line between yours and mine.
Psychologists tell us that boundaries are healthy to define the
scope of our commitments. It's good to set limits, I used to tell
my children, because limits provide support. To be bound also
means to be connected, as in "ties that bind." In the best of
times, the marriage vows that my husband and I promised
decades ago bind us; we are determined to live into the love
we pledged. Responsibilities embraced through vows contrast

ominously with the physical bondage of prisoners. Our penal
system controls the men and women in a world symbolized
by fettered legs and cuffed wrists, eerily recalling enslaved
Black ancestors. When people are bound hand and foot, there
is no escape. Responsibility has no meaning here. Prisoners
have no freedom. They must go where their captors force them
to go.

The Judeo-Christian Exodus-emancipation narrative reca-
pitulated for me every era of America's national pilgrimage
toward justice. Everywhere I found traces of its insidiously
captivating and distorting influence. Exodus should be a lib-
erating talisman because it signifies a covenantal relationship
between God and God's chosen people. It should be.

Covenant and mutual commitment might pave the way for
a graced future if we *Shema!* If only the nation would listen to
God's enduring offer of relationship. But the terms of the covenant and well-being that God promises require that the orphan,
the widow, and the outcast be fully welcomed into the national
community. Sadly, so much of America's story centers on
exclusion and exploitation rather than covenantal justice. Our
cultural sin binds us. Racism binds us in America. It is our
original sin.

Moment 6: Origins and Original Sin

A couple of years ago, awakening in breeze-stirred darkness,
I savored the beginning of a new day on a different pilgrim
trail. Our class from the Jesuit School of Theology was hiking
in the footsteps of St. Ignatius in Catalonia along the Pyrenees
foothills. As day broke, I tuned in to the muffled murmurings
of fellow hikers rustling in their sleeping bags and drawing
one last, deep breath of oblivion. Their hushed tones sounded
to me like a wind shushing in the night, foretelling the dawning light that would stir the world into life. Before accompany-
ing the Jesuit School pilgrims on the *Camino Ignaciano*, I had
never anticipated sleeping in cramped hostel bunks shrouded

by damp clothes hung on every protruding peg. But on the trail, exhaustion-induced sleep washed the pungent odor of other *peregrinos* out of my worrying brain. When we awoke for another simmering day on the trail, the glimmering eastern horizon buoyed us anew. I trusted that, as "in the beginning," the night's deep shadows would yield to a new day's promise of sacred encounter.

Other dawns have not been so muted or meditative. Many years ago, my husband and I would startle awake with new-parent pounding hearts when our infant daughter clamored for yet another feeding. Gradually her gasping breaths would quiet as she nursed. She made satisfied sucking sounds, so trusting, so safe in my arms. We sighed collectively, hoping for all good blessings for her. Beginnings are always holy experiences—mysterious dawn-promises when the day or a child's life is unformed, undecided, and untainted. Origins mean promise.

Genesis, the first book of the Hebrew Scriptures, also stirs people's hopes with beginning promises. It narrates a more radical beginning—the dawn of time and space as our faith ancestors understood the origin of creation itself. "In the beginning, when God created the heavens and the earth, the earth was a formless wasteland, and darkness covered the face of the deep, while a mighty wind swept over the waters" (Gen 1:1-2). The "face of the deep" is often translated as "abyss" to signify a yawning emptiness at the dawn of creation. Emptiness is a not-yet-called-into-being state. Emptiness holds forth the possibility of new life, like a woman's womb. I imagine the creation abyss as an eternal wellspring of all that might be. Without specific form, the abyss is a sacred, mysterious dawn-space from which divine love and purpose radiate into life. In the Christian tradition, we say God created the cosmos *ex nihilo*—out of nothing—by speaking through the Word. God called the light of creation into being and judged creation to be good. As people of faith, we read Genesis for the wisdom and transcendent truths it reveals. We read it not to learn about the big bang or the first milliseconds of a universe coming into being. We read Genesis and the Hebrew Scriptures to imbibe wisdom that has endured millennia of human testing. Our origin is God. God is the source of being. All that exists, particularly humanity, is good—like God.

Every day, starting from an original daybreak still point, we rise for a holy, hopeful journey. And then yesterday's strife immediately greets our waking eyes. We recollect where we are and what's ahead. Life's demands fracture a languid, peaceful dawn and launch a flurry of anxious activity. Just as we begin the day or a project, something goes awry. One wrong cut or misstep seems to dim the hopes that had sustained us when we woke. In the *Miserere*, the psalmist's lament expresses humanity's daily remorse with the self-accusing refrain: "For I know my transgressions, / and my sin is ever before me. . . . Indeed, I was born guilty, / a sinner, when my mother conceived me" (vv. 3, 5). Our own transgressions taint the God-created goodness of our lives. The psalmist's words—"my sin is ever before me"—attest to the reality of original sin. Original sin expresses why the past haunts us, why people don't awake to the clean slate that we expect at each dawn.

The Genesis story of Eve and Adam in the Garden of Eden follows in the Bible right after the descriptions of creation. Some Christians retell the fall as a cautionary tale about disobedience. Our fabled parents acted on their own inclinations to eat the "forbidden fruit." They disobeyed God. God punished them with expulsion from the Garden followed by laborious lives and inevitable death. This summary interpretation is harmfully simplistic. I can't picture a tyrant God who demands because-I-say-so obedience and consigns misbehavers to eternal torture. There is more to the story of the Garden than that.

Because we know that Adam and Eve were not actual people, we also recognize that Genesis is not describing a historical event. Original sin is not a factual episode but a truth about humankind's alienation from God. Humanity's sin is not eat-ing the forbidden fruit; it's not even the disobedience in itself. Genesis offers a profound insight into human nature, as true now as it was three thousand years ago: our fundamental sin has always been about rejecting God. We estrange ourselves from God; we separate ourselves from each other. We reject God's justice as the way of life for our community. We decide not to live with neighbors in just relationships. We exclude others and draw lines between who is our neighbor and who is a stranger. We also draw moral judgment lines of good and bad, color lines. This estrangement burdens people's relationships over and over again, not as just one past setback but continuously. Original sin expresses the truth that our past choices bind our present realities. Good choices create the possibility of other good choices, but equally true, unjust and unloving choices create unjust, painful, or hate-filled consequences. A world devised on our own terms, not according to God's love and justice, is bound to fail. Once the divisions are in place, it becomes more and more difficult to right ourselves and repair the relationship. This is original sin.

It's been widely pronounced that racism is America's original sin.[18] This means, then, that we made terrible, fateful choices at the founding of our nation. The repercussions of those choices reverberate in suffering and distortion through the centuries. My experiences on this color-line pilgrimage verified this truth for me—over and over again. Racism is America's original sin.

Despite our sin, I also glimpsed moments of grace. Grace is God's presence and goodness, which we express in aligning ourselves with God. Grace is God's goodness poured into our hearts and relationships over and over again, unceasingly. Grace names God's relentless generosity toward us. There was

---

[18] Jim Wallis's book *America's Original Sin: Racism, White Privilege, and the Bridge to a New America* (Ada, MI: Brazos Press, 2016) is often cited as a contemporary source for this expression, but many other Christians working on anti-racism have long used the phrase.

no single historical fall of humanity from grace. Every day, tragically, we choose to reject God. Every day, fortunately, God as both Spirit and Redeemer invites us back into relationship and works for our reconciliation. We are called to heal this nation according to God's offer of a just relationship. There is no going back to a time before America's color line, but a graced future may be possible.

Shema, O Israel! Hear and respond! Love God with all your being and love your neighbor as yourself.

Moment 7: It's Not Just Black and White

On the verge of a pilgrim's path recollecting America's original sin, I needed to get my bearings on one last thing, like one last check of the map. What was I actually looking for? *Shema!* But pay attention to what? Race is not a simple black-and-white idea. It shadows everything in this nation. Everything.

I've had some personal experience with Black and white categories. I'm labeled white because my ancestry is so clearly from Europe, but my love binds me to people whom society labels Black. My husband is labeled Black because his features clearly show his African ancestry. Our children are "mixed" because people cannot decide how to label them. My husband and children have been hurt, our family has been wounded, by stinging words, intimidation, and lost chances because we are not abiding by the color line. Many people of color have similar stories of loss and suffering because of America's color line, much more profound than ours. Such experiences are tragic and humiliating, life threatening and unfair, frightening or perplexing—all because America's basic social category is a color line that separates who counts from who doesn't.

The boundary of the color line in this country is arbitrary because race labels are more than skin deep. The labels are tied not only to physical features like hair, skin color, and facial structures. The labels ride on cues about genetic ancestry. However, they are weighted with judgments about culture and connections, like speech patterns, clothing, grooming, income, and education. My children are hard for people to classify because their physical ancestry is so uncertain, not clearly from (or mostly from) Europe or Africa. Perfect strangers have demanded that they justify themselves: "*What* are you?" The implicit question, silent but high stakes, is whether they count as white or Black. It's hard to fathom why a genetic lottery determines their social value. Who gets to say?

I've finally found helpful ideas to express the complexities of racial labeling in the United States: a caste system. Isabel Wilkerson wrote: "The hierarchy of caste is not about feelings or morality. It is about power—which groups have it and which do not. It is about resources . . . who gets to acquire and control them and who does not. It is about respect, authority and assumptions of competence—who is accorded these and who is not."[19] Caste in any society is about social power. When we categorize someone according to their race in the United States, we make a judgment about their access to resources, respect, and life opportunities. "Racial categories are the products of politics and culture, not biology and nature. The idea that there are discrete, organic categories of black people and white people has been revealed by history and science to be a total fiction."[20] The American racial caste system remains firmly in place, according benefits and burdens simply because of the social place assigned to individuals, regardless of whether people intend these outcomes or not. Race matters because the United States is not a colorblind society but a caste-based hierarchy.

While America's original sin fetters us today, I hope that the country might, just might, break out of those fetters. Incidents like this one give me hope: In the months before his death in

---

[19] Isabel Wilkerson, *Caste: The Origins of Our Discontents* (New York: Random House, 2020), 17–18.
[20] Proenza-Coles, *American Founders*, xxxi–xxxii.

2013, my father was recounting the events that shaped his life. One story stood out. It had felt like a prophetic moment to him even a lifetime after it had happened. When I was five years old, our family sailed across the Atlantic. We were five children, and my mother was pregnant with another baby when the ocean liner docked in Sicily for my father's Fulbright semester at the University of Messina. Since his emphasis was on American legal philosophy, many of his encounters with Italian law students centered on the Civil Rights Movement in the United States, particularly its impact on the South. At an evening lecture, a curious student interrogated him: "Would you let your daughter marry a Black man?" Before the U.S. Supreme Court's 1967 decision in *Loving v. Virginia*, state criminal laws in over half of the United States outlawed intermarriage across race lines. My father responded with humble honesty: "I hope I'll have the integrity to live by my principles . . . when that day comes." Fast forward fifteen years. I brought my future husband home to meet my parents and many siblings. He's an African American man whom I met when we were Yale undergraduates together. It seemed to me that my parents never flinched as they welcomed him and trusted him with their blue-eyed daughter. They loved their son-in-law generously and graciously, holding him tightly in their hearts, until their deaths decades later. Our beloved children were joined over the years by many other rainbow cousins, and over the years, many other families like ours have formed in this country. Is it possible to hope that the color line is receding? On this pilgrimage, the answer came to me: Yes. And no.

Getting My Bearings

In the triple reckonings of 2020, America's original sin came into sharper and sharper focus for the nation as a whole. It became impossible to ignore. In the reckoning moment as I started this odyssey, I began to grasp how American lives are hobbled with the full-shackled legacy of past choices and current complicity in an unjust racial caste system. We live and move handcuffed all together. I realized that the only way forward was to look backward—to recollect America's original sin—and then respond with a grace-converted heart. This would be my pilgrim's path. "Have mercy on me, O God, / according to your steadfast love" (Ps 51:1).

My armchair pilgrimage started slowly as I got my bearings. I planned my route, took up my shillelagh, and grabbed my prayers on the threshold of this color-line *camino*. As I stepped out, I tallied the nuggets of wisdom that I had collected to sustain me on the path. First, the point of pilgrimage was to enter a sacred space with my ego defenses down so I could listen. *Shema!* The journey would be messy, like life, with moments of swirling chaos and moments of soaring promise. Moments on this pilgrimage would be abhorrent and heartbreaking; encounters on this pilgrimage would reveal deep courage in lives sacrificed for freedom. Second, I trusted that God's grace would lead me as an openhearted pilgrim. During the first week's trekking, I experienced a small sense of reassurance. It was not that the path would be easy but that the pilgrimage would offer grace for justice. "The sacrifice acceptable to God is a broken spirit; / a broken and contrite heart, O God, you will not despise" (Ps 51:17).

I prayed that, by leaning on Psalm 51's words of wisdom, my father's walking stick, and the Shema prayer, I would find a way to grasp God's wisdom "in my secret heart" (Ps 51:6). At the close of this week, I crossed the threshold and headed to New Orleans along the Mississippi River to listen for stories there. Civil Rights hero Vincent Harding observed: "There is something deeply built into us that needs story itself. . . . [W]e cannot become really true human beings for ourselves and for each other without story."[21] He called the witnesses who shared their stories "signposts." Signposts are human

---

[21] Vincent Harding, interview by Krista Tippett, "Our Lives Can Be Signposts for What's Possible," *The On Being Project*, NPR, May 13, 2019, https://onbeing.org/programs/vincent-harding-is-america-possible/.

beings whose stories direct us toward wiser lives if we choose to listen. The moments of the second week in Louisiana, I knew, would bring me face to face with people who were shackled and forced to labor on plantations. I knew I would encounter the living legacy of America's original sin. More than seeing the sights, I planned to listen for stories and look for signposts.

Shema! Walk with me.

Second Week
Shackled Past and Present in Louisiana

During the second week on pilgrimage I explored Louisiana, figuratively a hop, skip, and jump in time and distance from our country's East Coast colonial origins. While the regional cultures differed, both were bound by our nation's deep-rooted racial caste hierarchy. In the moments of this week, the country's nineteenth-century slaveholding society built upon chattel slavery was still in plain view in Louisiana. The country's past still shackled African Americans; it shackles all Americans.

Before this color-line pilgrimage, New Orleans and Louisiana had refused my efforts to box them, safe and sound, into domesticated sketches. The humidity, heat, and hurricane-threatened bayous formed tangled, damp impressions in my mind. The region also sparkled, beckoning me like colorful and dangerous glass shards. Before this pilgrimage, I had known only bits and pieces about this paradoxical delta city that has lived so tantalizingly large in the national imagination. I had gathered all sorts of facts and facile judgments from TV, online media, and friends' vacation reports. Picture-perfect ads of New Orleans had tempted me to saunter through the French Quarter as a place of gaudy Mardi Gras celebrations promising bacchanalian release from the drudgery of northern winters. Jazz was born here, as were all the musical genres so distinctively American: the blues, Negro spirituals, rock and roll, and hip hop. Its cuisine and place names revealed its French and Creole history. Preparing for this week's trekking, I realized finally what unnerved me in the menacing memories

33

and sharp, splintered tales that I had collected about New Orleans: with the proverbial log in my eye, I had not wanted to confront New Orleans and Louisiana because recollections of terrible racial violence there frightened me.

My itinerary this week led me first to New Orleans proper. Its past was cached in restored historic buildings, burrowed in the land's vegetation and marshes, and narrated in the residents' speech and customs. To trace the color line running through the region, I began on the banks of the Mississippi River near the port. Then, past the ironwork and alleys of the French Quarter, I recollected the *communitas* echoes of drum celebrations, which had pulsed in Congo Square's foot-pounded dirt commons. On an upriver plantation museum, now tranquil, I faced the reality of enslaved human beings' short, brutal lives that unexpectedly intersected my own. I paused to excavate the Catholic presence in the region. My own faith ancestors both shamefully sinned against their fellow human beings and audaciously triumphed over the surrounding sin-soaked culture. The last moment of this week allowed me to pause in the Lower Ninth Ward under the levees' ominous shadow. Here was the legacy of enslavement, presenting itself as poverty and social abandonment as Black residents demanded that America fulfill its promises to them.

To grasp America's original sin, I had to pay attention to what happened in the Deep South along the Mississippi River two hundred years ago, so I begged God's grace for a wide-open heart. Defended with my father's shillelagh, girded with my penitential prayer, and steeled for the unpredictable, I journeyed to New Orleans to reckon with its past—with our country's past. I was surprised by what I discovered this week about our nation and myself. *Shema!* Walk with me!

Moment 1: Sold Down the River

Standing early on a Saturday morning at a broad bend on the murky Mississippi's east bank, I tentatively breathed in the mild fall air. The Mississippi River flowed from its far-north source in Minnesota south over two thousand miles to the Gulf Coast. It marked the boundary between the country's British-settled states and the French territorial expanse that Jefferson purchased for the United States in 1803. French explorers settled the Gulf Coast from east to west and asserted ownership over the vast Mississippi watershed for France. The sprawling settlements of New Orleans from its earliest days have flourished for centuries a few miles inland from the wide flat delta where river and land mingle. From the river's edge at the Jackson Square landing, I looked west to Algiers Point, where the trans-atlantic slaving ships had disgorged their human cargo.[1] Enslaved individuals were then bound away to the French Quarter for sale. Today, anguished moans no longer floated on the wind. I saw only an incongruous assortment of riverfront hotels, high-rise buildings, and tricked-out steamboats with their layered decks. These hardly squared with the ships that once docked there with kidnapped cargo in their holds. To the south of Jackson Square, I saw seemingly innocuous industrial cranes thrusting their white skeletons skyward to load and unload ships crammed with ever-changing payloads.

---

[1] The *Slave Voyages* database documents over 325,000 men, women, and children who had been shipped legally and illegally to the North American coast during the centuries of the transatlantic slave trade—mostly to the Carolinas, to the Chesapeake Bay region, and in lesser numbers, to Canada. Researchers estimate that over 12 million Africans in total were transported for enslavement on the American continents and the Caribbean islands, one of the largest forced migrations in human history. Approximately 95% of all Africans disembarked in the Caribbean and South America, 4% in North America, and the rest in Europe. Records document that, in 1719, the first two ships originating from the west coast of Africa carried kidnapped individuals to Louisiana; over 100,000 people were eventually sold as chattel to labor on land and in cities in Louisiana before the Emancipation Proclamation. "Explore the Dispersal of Enslaved Africans across the Atlantic World," *Slave Voyages*, accessed February 15, 2021, https://slavevoyages.org/.

> "Moans are the utterance of choice when circumstances snatch words and prayers from bereft lips. As time went on, the moans from the slave ship's cargo hold lost their human sound, for there is no bodily response that could assuage or comfort, no sound that could fully express the horror. If there were such a sound or expression adequate to the task, it would break the hearts of all who heard it."
>
> Barbara Holmes, *Joy Unspeakable*[2]

"Sold down the river" expresses betrayal. It's a casual expression signifying dismay when our friends or family members have not supported us as we expected. We rarely pause over its origins when we complain that life's deck has been stacked against us. "Sold down the river" actually refers to this country's shameful, shrouded but well-developed business of transporting enslaved people inland to plantations distant from the East Coast ports. The "inland slave trade," as it had been called, flourished right up to the Civil War. The practice of selling kidnapped and enslaved persons down the river began in earnest in 1808 after the international community banned the transatlantic trade. Thus, breeding and transporting people for forced labor within the South became a lucrative industry in itself. It generated profits to salvage the declining fortunes of the Eastern Seaboard's landed gentry. In the nineteenth century, New Orleans was one of the largest marketplaces for purchasing enslaved laborers.

The betrayal of being "sold down the river" captured the experience of Africans and their descendants in the Upper South of Virginia and Maryland. The threat of sale was psychological torture sometimes used as a threat to control unruly laborers, but tragically, it was too often a reality. Black people,

[2] Barbara A. Holmes, *Joy Unspeakable: Contemplative Practices of the Black Church* (Minneapolis: Fortress Press, 2017), 49–50.

enslaved or free, were ripped without warning from their families to be sold down the river. Some were kidnapped, others were traded by white families who owned them. All were sold to drivers whose only job was to move the human chattel to the marketplaces further west and further south. Whipped along a trail of tears out of Alexandria, Richmond, or Norfolk,[3] they trudged in coffle lines, dozens of human beings chained by their legs and necks. Scarcely protected from cold and heat, they trekked mile after mile. Seeking the most profit possible, drivers force-marched men, women, and children across the Blue Ridge Mountains of Virginia, across the song-celebrated Shenandoah River. People were shipped down the Ohio and the Mississippi Rivers, to Deep South auction blocks. Louisville and Natchez were departure ports for flatbeds and steamboats bound for New Orleans with their human cargo. Researchers estimate that nearly a million enslaved laborers from Virginia and Maryland were driven further south and inland to enrich plantation owners during the agricultural boom and bust cycles of the nineteenth century. The height of the trade coincided with the settlement of the Louisiana Territory, land lust fueled by sparkling promises of wealth in the lawless infancy of global market economies and the rise of corporations. Even though northern states had abolished slavery, their factory towns flourished on the backs of crops produced by human chattel.

A bit further along the riverbank in New Orleans, I studied the tall bronze marker near the public sidewalk that tallied for tourists what had happened here. The marker for the "Transatlantic Slave Trade to Louisiana" recounted this history in a

---

[3] Edward Ball, "Slavery's Trail of Tears: Retracing America's Forgotten Migration," *Smithsonian* 46, no. 7 (November 2015): 58–83. For this moment, I also relied on Edward Baptist's extensive research and rigorous analysis of the inland slave trade in the U.S. and the conditions of enslaved individuals' lives in *The Half Has Never Been Told: Slavery and the Making of American Capitalism* (New York: Basic Books, 2016).

single central icon emblazoned with the widely recognized
Pan-African colors: yellow, red, and green. A canary-yellow
circle surrounded a heart-shaped image of the sankofa bird.
The bird twisted its head backward toward its tail, retrieving
a precious egg. *Sankofa* from Ghanaian tribal languages trans-
lates to "go back and get it." It symbolized that communities
would be stronger when they retrieved and retained their
ancestral values. The stylized bird was superimposed upon a
dramatic red outline of Louisiana within the boundaries of
Africa, the continent colored in vibrant green. The text below
the icon related a few summary details of Louisiana's participation in the transatlantic slave trade, recording the tribes,
genders, and ages of the Africans who were carried to this port
against their wills.

The concrete amphitheater beside the Moonwalk pedestrian
path offered me on that morning a cool, sturdy seat where I
could rest and remember the souls who had passed through
here in shackles. My heart felt like the braided weeds I saw on
the dismal mudbank as the waves tugged at their stems. I was
restless as my mind snagged on thoughts that were too much
to take in.

Sankofa. Do we treasure our past? I mused to myself when
I considered sankofa wisdom in the context of U.S. culture.
Mostly, it seemed to me that people in the United States value
being unfettered and free from their past. They treasure being
an individual who can progress unfettered into the future.
Ideas of freedom have changed in this nation since its founding. Thoughts of escape and a brave new world of freedom
sustained British Puritans crossing the ocean as they dreamed
of creating a shining city on the hill. They framed their story
as God's deliverance from tyranny to liberty, an Exodus. At
first reflection, Exodus seemed to be solely about emancipation, meaning to be free from the demands of overlords or
monarchs. I knew that such a characterization of Exodus was
too simple and pat. My faith understanding told me that
Exodus was about fidelity—fidelity to relationships—much
more than about being unfettered.

The Hebrew Scriptures' Exodus drama is not history, precisely (although archeological evidence of the rise and fall of ancient Semitic tribes at the eastern end of the Mediterranean Sea aligns with the timeline laid out in Exodus). Rather, the drama recounts the Israelites' exciting escape from Egypt. Jewish tradition celebrates the Exodus events through ritualized Passover practices to remember how Yahweh saved them and formed them into God's own people. The Israelites' bondage started centuries before their enslavement in Egypt prompted them to call upon God: *"Shema!* Listen to our calls and save us!"* Speaking for God to the pharaoh, Moses demanded: "Let my people go!" The angel of God executed all firstborn males in Egypt but "passed over" the Israelites, who had marked their lintels with sacrificial blood. Escaping in the confusing aftermath of widespread death, Moses led the people across the Red Sea's windswept bed, while the pharaoh's army drowned behind them in the crashing waters. Following this dramatic liberation, the Israelites roamed for forty years through the Sinai desert wilderness before they reached the banks of the Jordan River. God provided daily manna, nightly quails, and rock-sourced water to sustain the tribes. God and the Israelites sealed the Torah covenant on Mount Sinai, which memorialized their mutual and everlasting commitment to full fidelity and trust.

I felt kinship with the Israelites, who wandered forty years through a liminal desert space to meet God. Forty is a holy God-quantity in the Judeo-Christian Scriptures. With grace, deserts are paradigmatic settings where a person can wrestle with God and find transformation. In the Exodus desert adventure, God formed a collection of individuals from kin into covenanted community. In the long, holy pause between their enslaved past and their promised-land future, God and the Israelites pledged fidelity to each other: "I will take you as my people, and I will be your God" (Exod 6:7). The terms of the holy covenant became the Torah, the law that would govern the people's relationships. *Berit* is often translated from Hebrew into English as covenant or contract, but its literal meaning is "shackle" or "chain." The Ten Commandments dictated how the people would live bound together in covenant with God in the promised land. The commandments have been summarized throughout the centuries in two brief imperatives: love God and love your neighbor.

I was struck then by the essence of Exodus: Yahweh liberated Israel from slavery to the pharaoh so that they would be shackled to each other and to God's own self: "Remember the long way that the LORD your God has led you these forty years in the wilderness, in order to humble you, testing you to know what was in your heart, whether or not you would keep his commandments. He humbled you . . . in order to make you understand that one does not live by bread alone, but by every word that comes from the mouth of the LORD" (Deut 8:2-3). The Torah was the ligature identity—the *re-ligio*—that bound them together, past, present, and future.

Musings on Exodus brought me back to sankofa wisdom. To be liberated is to be emancipated from constraints for a purpose. God liberated the Israelites so that they would live in a community grounded in justice for a shared future. This aligned with sankofa. Sankofa meant to me that we could not separate ourselves from our sisters and brothers or from our past, especially the human relationship binding us as one. Relationships with other people are the only possible foundation for our lives. The meanings of sankofa and Exodus came together in my mind.

I stirred myself from my reverie, ready to meet New Orleans. In the benign sunshine, the silent, ever-flowing water restored some calm to my searching thoughts. The deep brown river's flow, gliding smoothly past, and the sparkling water itself seemed to offer a solemn tribute to the stolen lives and labor that built New Orleans and our nation. The great river's steady flow carried the past pain out to sea in a holy ritual of cleansing.

Psalm 51 again voiced my repentant plea before God: "Wash me thoroughly from my iniquity, / and cleanse me from my sin. / For I know my transgressions; / my sin is ever before me" (vv. 2-3). I understood that I needed to face the sin that still shackled our nation, the sin which has always been plainly before us. If I wanted to be a part of a community of faithful justice, I needed to face the full story of America's original sin and sift everything with the grace of sankofa wisdom.

Moment 2: The Past Is Present in New Orleans

I turned from the river to the city. My steps led me in this moment from the French Quarter past the auction-block marker of the slave exchange, past the Tomb of the Unknown Slave, and over to Congo Square. All around me, I glimpsed evidence of the country's dark history even in the bright morning sunshine. I tried to pay attention and absorb what I experienced. As well as I could, I practiced *Shema!* and attempted to follow God's command.

The French Quarter: The crowded sidewalks on both sides of the French Quarter's narrow streets overwhelmed me. Tourists wandered, stopping and starting unpredictably, and music congested the air. Along with my feet, my thoughts stumbled at every new crossing as I tried to decipher the past hidden beneath ornately reconstructed building facades. During the antebellum period, this neighborhood housed one of the highest concentrations of millionaires in the South. Perhaps I should not have been surprised at the magnitude of money in a slave-market city. Wealth and oppression go hand in hand; labor exploitation has so often been the mechanism by which governments secure extreme wealth for a privileged class of people.

Only a mile distant from the riverfront, the streets were awash—brimming—with racial and social complexity. The street names proclaimed New Orleans's French and Catholic lineage. St. Louis, St. Ann, and St. Peter Streets crossed the city, perpendicular to the Mississippi, from the river toward Tremé-Lafitte. Rampart Street and Barracks Street recorded the fortifications that once protected New Orleans from enemies storming up from the riverbank. Bourbon Street, named after the French ruling family in the early eighteenth century, and Dumaine Street, for the illegitimate son of Louis XIV, proclaimed their former royal alliances. These names sounded stilted in my broad eastern-midwestern accent. My speech marked me as an outsider, which is how I felt. But a foreigner, a saunterer without a place in this world (*sans terre*), can make connections that might have eluded the residents, who are too accustomed to what has been.

Even when the young United States nation purchased the Louisiana Territory in 1803, all shades of humanity destined for all walks of life mingled together in this delta city. The people who sauntered in the French Quarter were labeled according to the strains of their ancestry with terms like "quadroon," "octoroon," or simply "mulatto," meaning mixed. Such color labels, based more on culture and custom than genetic reality, served to segment and calculate human value. The people who owned other human beings might have been of African or European descent, but for enslaved individuals the color of their skin mattered; it constrained them and condemned them. An expression like "high yellow," still in use today, signaled the stigma of African descent while paradoxically elevating an individual's light skin. Some people of color were able to "pass" as white, because onlookers judged them by their fair skin and European features. While passing might have seemed to be a good-luck chance, it was risky and always entailed heartbreaking alienation and isolation.

There was no such thing as being colorblind in New Orleans back in the day—or now, either. Societies have always drawn lines of social distinction. For example, in ancient Palestine, Jews drew a bright line between neighbor and Samaritan. The surprise of Jesus' story about the good Samaritan is that a reviled stranger could act with more compassion and justice than one of the chosen people. In America, we look to people's skin color to know where to place them on the hierarchy of caste and virtue. I remembered my three-year-old daughter's first lesson on the importance of color. Her father went to pick her up one day from nursery school. His skin and features had always been labeled Black, while hers were more ambiguous, with her light tan skin, blond hair, and blue eyes. That afternoon, she stood behind her teacher in the classroom doorway, clamoring for notice: "My dad is here! He's right there!" Even though her father was the only parent in the lobby, wearing his suit and tie from the office, the teacher wouldn't release his own daughter into his care. "There's no one there, honey," the teacher reprimanded our tearful child. In America, past and present, to be Black has meant to be invisible; it has meant that a person does not count.

> "I'm mixed with the bravery of a soldier and the passion of activists. I'm mixed with the rage of a victim and the hope of a survivor. I'm mixed with the brilliance of a polymath and the swag of a 'hood boy.' I'm mixed with the past and present and my future is as bright as my skin. I'm mixed, because I'm both spiritual and human and my life is both joyous and challenging. . . . What am I mixed with you ask? I'm mixed with great thought and measured action, which is helping to create a world where one day people will ask 'How are you doing?' before asking 'What are you mixed with?'"
>
> Christopher Norris,
> "The Question I'm Often Asked as a 'High Yellow' Black Man"[4]

Aware of this as I toured the French Quarter, I watched for the nineteenth-century contributions of enslaved Africans and their descendants, contributions that might otherwise have been invisible. The French Quarter has traded on the tangled beauty of its wrought iron decorations, evident everywhere.

---

[4] Christopher Norris, "The Question I'm Often Asked as a 'High Yellow' Black Man," *The Good Men Project*, 2021, https://goodmenproject.com/featured-content/cnorris-the-question-im-often-asked-as-a-high-yellow-black-man/.

I appreciated the iron gates and fences that adorned the
St. Louis Cathedral. The graceful church occupied a place of
pride in the neighborhood because its triple spires were visible
above the rooftops. Rebuilt at the end of the eighteenth century
after a devastating fire, the cathedral claimed to be the oldest
in North America. On the morning I visited, its white sun-
sparkling facade was set off against manicured lawns and tall
lampposts, segmenting a delicate, black iron fence. Elsewhere
in the Quarter, above pedestrians' heads, a parade of balconies
also flaunted elegant wrought iron railings.

West African blacksmiths, either free or enslaved, had forged
iron into ornate scrolls, with webs of filigree and complicated
flourishes. Many blacksmiths had their signature motifs, such
as acorns, oak leaves, or intertwined vines, still on display
centuries later, though now refurbished with brightly painted
colors. Architectural historians read dramas from the balconies'
designs, finding the initials of the families who had lived there
and indications of whether there were marriageable daughters
in the house. Some designs subtly proclaimed resistance to
white-dominated society with rebellious meanings hidden in
an artisan's tribal symbols. However, historical markers rarely
acknowledged the enslaved craftsmen whose pounding labor
created the city's unparalleled grandeur. I also remembered,
as I resumed my sauntering, that blacksmithing skills produced shackles and leg-irons as well as delicate iron filigree.

St. Louis Hotel: Moving inland from the river, like a gawking
tourist rather than a wisdom-seeking pilgrim, I photographed
the marker identifying the St. Louis Hotel. The hotel had
hosted one of the largest and most well-known auction blocks
in the United States, the end of the line for the coffle-chained
gangs sold down the river. Other markers in New Orleans
recounted that captives awaiting sale had been penned in
"Negro yards" all over the city. They were forced to display
themselves in the stockade lots in a devilish mimicry of a liturgical procession. Beatings and threats had forced them to
participate in their own sale, by greasing their skins, demon-

strating their agility, or exaggerating their skills. I nearly over-looked the fading sign of the New Orleans Exchange on the outside wall of the Omni Royale Orleans Hotel near the park-ing garage. All that remained visible on the wall was the half-word "CHANGE" to mark the anguish that had hung in that place here two hundred years ago.

In color drawings of the time, now preserved, the hotel's soaring rotunda was depicted as uplifting, light filled, and gracious. One drawing I examined showed bound, naked, and desperate dark-skinned women and men under the dome. On the periphery, neck-ruffled white people drank tea, ironically unruffled by the human trauma in their midst.[5] Advertise-ments from the period contributed chilling details about auc-tion practices. One notice from March 1858 described eight people for sale from Alabama by name, age, coloring, skills, and defects, such as burns or lost fingers. A whole family was listed: George, 23, "carriage driver, very likely and intelligent"; his wife Martha, 30, a cook and laundress; and their four chil-dren, Ned—7, Nancy—6, Horace—4, and Mary—18 months.[6] "Very likely" meant tractable, obedient. Enslaved people were valued according to how much labor could be extracted from their limbs. Individuals in the prime of life were most valuable. The price for men was greater than for women. Women, however, could be bred to produce children, adding to an en-slaver's wealth through more field hands or as inventory for sale. Laborers who were scarred by whip strokes or rebellion brands commanded a lesser price because they were obviously difficult to control. Field hands were less valuable than domes-tic servants with cooking or housekeeping skills. Captive men and women with rarer expertise in sugar-making, carpentry,

---

[5] Brett Todd, Kate Mason, and Kathryn O'Dwyer, eds., "St. Louis Hotel & Exchange: Auctioning Off Lives," *New Orleans Historical*, accessed February 15, 2021, https://neworleanshistorical.org/items/show/926.

[6] "Slave Sale Advertisement," 1858, *New Orleans Historical*, accessed Febru-ary 15, 2021, https://neworleanshistorical.org/items/show/1370.

cooperage, and tailoring commanded commensurately higher prices.

In encountering tales of the auction blocks in New Orleans, I heard a phrase that made me shudder. At that time, just as now, women and Black people had been subjugated, considered suitable to be dominated and used as white men's property. The New Orleans slaveholding society perceived Black women's bodies in particular as property for white men's sexual satisfaction. Attractive "Negro women" of fair complexion were in demand as concubines and prostitutes in New Orleans brothels. White men bought and sold the women as "fancy girls." The phrase struck a nerve, pointing to a connection that I hardly dared to acknowledge. "Fancy girls" was the nickname our daughters gave themselves when they played dress-up years ago. "Mom, you're so lucky to have us—your fancy girls!" Had we lived two hundred years ago in New Orleans, our daughters would have most likely faced a life of satisfying white men's sexual desires simply because of their African heritage. They might have been fancy girls.

Congo Square: From the horrors of the auction blocks, I paced somberly toward Congo Square. The autumn afternoon was bright, but the still-lush fall canopy offered me shade for solace and sanctuary from the Quarter's hive of activity. The Tremé-Lafitte neighborhood surrounded the park. It had once been sacred Houma Indian land before becoming a plantation that produced food for city dwellers in the late 1700s. Tremé-Lafitte of centuries past had sheltered individuals of color of all statuses: free people, those enslaved to white or mulatto city residents, and Africans recently disembarked. Narrow shotgun-style houses with Caribbean and African architectural details still dotted its streets. The Tomb of the Unknown Slave beside St. Augustine Church had anchored this mixed-ancestry neighborhood since the nineteenth century.[7] The monument's cross

[7] Christina Lawrence, "St. Augustine Catholic Church," *New Orleans Historical*, accessed February 15, 2021, https://neworleanshistorical.org/items/show/551.

of rusting iron chains honored slaves whose deaths (from violence, overwork, or age) had been unmarked and unremarked. The sacred soil here absorbed the blood and tears of human beings too long deemed expendable. As I passed, I prayed silently for absolution and a path to forgiveness so that our sinning nation could return to God's embrace. I knew our nation's sins would not be easily expiated.

"On this October 30, 2004, we, the Faith Community of St. Augustine Catholic Church, dedicate this shrine consisting of grave crosses, chains and shackles to the memory of the nameless, faceless, turfless Africans who met an untimely death in Faubourg Treme. . . . This St. Augustine/Treme shrine honors all slaves buried throughout the United States and those slaves in particular who lie beneath the ground of Treme, in unmarked, unknown graves. . . . The Church sits astride the blood, sweat, tears and some of the mortal remains of unknown slaves from Africa and local American Indian slaves. . . . The Tomb of the Unknown Slave is a constant reminder that we are walking on holy ground."

Excerpts from the public marker at the Tomb of the Unknown Slave

In Congo Square that afternoon, a few people milled around, strolling and chatting, persons of all descriptions and many accents. Bronze statues and contemporary art installments were situated along the walkways memorializing Louis Armstrong Park's vibrant musical and cultural history. In the mid-eighteenth century, however, hundreds of free and enslaved Africans would have gathered here at *Place des Nègres*. Even then, the unrelenting colorism of racial caste had shackled every moment of people's lives: Africans had gathered in *Place des Nègres*, but Afro-Creoles (those of African descent born in the United States) and "American slaves" from the Upper South were permitted to congregate at other public venues in the city, even in mixed-race ballrooms. The Africans who gathered at Congo Square hailed from Senegambia, a region along the African continent's western coast, although they claimed diverse tribal ancestries with different languages. Their shared experience as strangers kidnapped to a strange land offered a path toward community, a possibility of human companionship and acceptance in dark days.

Finding temporary freedom from white gazes, people gathered on the grassy field of *Place des Nègres* on Sundays—the only day granted for leisure under Louisiana's *Code Noir* ("Black Code"). The Congo Square community traded produce and household goods. People shared stories and embraced loved ones. Historical descriptions of the meadow have inevitably remarked upon the drumming and dancing circles that happened here. Drumming and dancing had a sacred cosmological significance for uprooted West Africans. Ritual drumming in community "draws the listener toward the sacred realm within and without. In the drum rhythms, ancestors hear and remember their responsibilities to the living; the living hear the beating heart of the ongoing universe and reorder their priorities so that their life energy is attuned to the pulse of life."[8] Drumming and dancing were salvation practices. On the transatlantic passage, the captives were forced to dance on the ship decks in a perversion of their past lives. Drummers beat out rhythms of remembrance and resistance. Dancers stepped in time, using their bodies to communicate lament and suffering that were deeper than words could express. Drumming was never about entertainment for Africans caught in the inhuman business of chattel slavery. In the presence of ancestors and ancestral gods, they forged fragile human bonds that kept their bodies and spirits alive for just another moment.

Scenes of the French Quarter and Congo Square, past and present, showed me the many ruses white people have used to erase the sin of chattel slavery from the story of our country's

[8] Holmes, *Joy Unspeakable*, 38.

history. A veneer of new place names, refurbished balconies, and modernized ports might sometimes obscure a region's past. But New Orleans of the nineteenth century had been a society founded on enslaved labor, no matter what moments of relief or beauty its streets offered me two hundred years later. America's original sin was still present.

The next shrine—unholy shrine—on my pilgrim's path was a sugarcane plantation just north of New Orleans, up the river. *Shema!* Walk with me.

Moment 3: Raising Cane

Of all the moments on this pilgrimage, the Whitney Plantation Museum represented for me a place and time nearly beyond the reach of even God's grace. In that moment, I met the memories of men, women, and children who had been fettered on the land raising cane in Louisiana a century and a half ago.

Plantations in the Louisiana Territory grew cane, indigo, and cotton as the most lucrative crops of the antebellum South.[9]

---

[9] Slavery was essential for the United States to achieve the economic, political, and social world dominance that our country enjoys today. It was a tragic "perfect storm" that birthed chattel slavery. Sugar cane cultivation arrived in Europe at the dawn of the modern era, coinciding with the age of transoceanic exploration. Once a luxury spice, sugar became a staple sweetener, and its value accelerated with international trade in tea, coffee, and chocolate. Limited liability corporations were ingenious financial and legal devices engineered to distribute cost and risk for far-flung ventures. The last necessary condition for the rise of chattel slavery was the appropriation of sparsely populated and easily conquered lands in the Western Hemisphere. Modern banking transactions, such as letters of credit, insurance, and mortgages, were developed to secure investors against the financial risk of selling perishable property in distant places on uncertain dates. In the United States, wealthy landowners in the southern states and factory owners in the northern states prospered handsomely from the plantation economy that emerged at this time in global history. European nations also profited richly from the plantation economies around the globe. See, generally, Ball, "Slavery's Trail of Tears"; Baptist, *Half Has Never Been Told*; and Christina Proenza-Coles, *American Founders: How People of African Descent Established Freedom in the New World* (Montgomery, AL: NewSouth Books, 2019).

Sugar cultivation became profitable in the late 1700s with the development of varieties that could be planted in early spring in temperate climates for a December harvest. The emergence of new varieties coincided fortuitously with the United States' purchase of the massive Louisiana Territory. The federal government offered land grants in the territory for plantation farms, which tempted all types of investors, farmers, and adventurers to seek their fortune by heading west and south. Most new plantation owners were white, some were free people of color, but all were demonically possessed with the prospect of getting rich from land and enslaved labor.

The Whitney Plantation Museum's mission today was to tell the story of plantation life from the perspective of enslaved individuals. The Haydel family owned the Whitney plantation for a century before the Civil War. Typically, as it was with Whitney, plantation acreage was laid out in a grid with narrow frontage along the Mississippi River and deep parcels stretching into swamps and bayous. River access reduced the costs of shipping sugar and cotton to market. Whitney's main approach when I visited was no longer the shaded, gracious oak-lined drive leading to the slaveholders' "big house"; instead, a simple gravel drive led to the back fields. As a ticketed visitor, I received a lanyard displaying the image of a bronze-cast statue honoring one of the "Children of the Whitney" that told of the child's life in the child's own words. The brief biographies, like the one of Frances on my lanyard, were culled from a Depression-era WPA oral history project that interviewed men, women, and children who had been freed by the Emancipation Proclamation. As I read Frances's story, the docent emphasized that "slaves" had not lived at Whitney, but *people* had been captured, traded, or bred for conscripted labor on this land. Slavery was their condition, not their identity.

The docent shared that more than twenty-five hundred individuals of all ages were enslaved at Whitney in the decades before the Civil War. Some were born on the estate, but a large percentage walked northward in shackles after being purchased at auction in New Orleans. To prosper, the plantation economy needed a continuous river of human labor because sugar cultivation was grueling. The laborers' lives were always precarious, sometimes only lasting four or five years, as they were forced to bring the plantation owners' sugar crop to market. Nevertheless, owners were able to cover the purchase price of each human laborer in that brief time because the labor was uncompensated—stolen. Often the overseers and slave drivers were themselves held captive and were forced to perform their brutal responsibilities. Their job was to manage the sugar production cycle by any means necessary.

"Saving up riches without regard for the other
We see it in the Gospels
We saw it on plantations
We saw it in lynchings
We saw it in the response to the Civil Rights Movement
We see it today
Monetary riches
Material riches
Emotional riches
Social riches
Awash in the blood of Black bodies"

Ellen Jewett, "Yet the Last Are Still Last"[10]

Sugar production began in early spring during bent-over weeks when field hands planted thick cane stalks in shallow furrows, acre by acre. After the young plants sprouted, the enslaved laborers had to fertilize the fields and keep them weed- and pest-free. Under the overseer's exacting eye, men and women harvested cane by machete just before the late fall

[10] Ellen Jewett, "Yet the Last Are Still Last," *New Horizons* 5, no. 1, art. 12 (2021). Used by permission.

frosts. Next, the most dangerous process began: to convert the cane-stalk bounty into granules of sugar before the crop rotted. Laborers stripped the razor-like leaves from each stalk, then chopped and pressed the stalks to extract the juice prize. Around-the-clock processing required every available worker to stir the boiling syrup until the moisture was released and the sweet remainder was packaged into hogshead barrels. The weathered iron cauldrons, with fierce fires below and scalding syrup within, were only one of the life-threatening menaces for adults and children laboring day and night to produce sugar.

It's little wonder that the enslaved workers at Whitney often died within a few years. The list of physical threats was horrifyingly long: shackle infections and lead poisoning, burns from syrup processing, infected skin wounds from sharp cane leaves or harvesting tools, mosquito-borne diseases, starvation, flogging, childbirth, and exhaustion. Rape and forced impregnation were for women common facts of life, often followed by the heartbreaking grief of their captors and rapists stealing their infants. Terror, grief, and desperation compounded individuals' bodily suffering—human beings died here because it was just too hard to live.

As I gazed upon the sugar fields, swatting bugs from my neck, an unnerving insight flashed in my mind: all of this human violence, all of this suffering, was greed driven. And then, another realization sent me reeling—my own story was closely connected to the story of sugarcane. My father grew up in his grandfather's house. He was a grandchild only three years younger than his aunt, treated like a son and a sibling. Many times, I had shared my family story by fitting it into the typical American Dream template. I recounted that my father was the first in his family to go to college. He married young, was a veteran, went to law school, and alongside his Catholic wife, raised nine healthy children. Not exactly rags to riches, but still it was a story of success based on hard work. I had thought that southern labor exploitation was not part of my story because my parents were New Yorkers.

I have learned that every American is shackled to chattel slavery in some way. All of us. Some of us, though, are closer than others. My Irish great-grandfather—my father's grand-father—was a sugar broker on Wall Street in the 1930s. He commuted into New York City on the Long Island Railroad from his spacious brick house in Rockville Centre. As a sugar broker, he facilitated market transactions between sugar grow-ers in the South and the refineries and food producers in the North. In that period, impoverished, land-shackled Black sharecroppers labored in the cane fields across Louisiana and other southern states. Brutal work conditions prevailed, while pervasive poverty crippled their families. President Franklin Roosevelt's New Deal policies, a safety net for white Ameri-cans after the war, provided no protection for them. They were excluded from Social Security, worked without minimum wages or union protections, and were subjected to Jim Crow terrors. Because my great-grandfather's safe and settled life relied on exploited labor, our family story was not the unadul-terated proof of the American Dream that I thought it was. It was a story of working hard, but it also exemplified how white advancement rides on the backs of people of color, regardless of whether we know it or choose it. All of us in this nation, across the rainbow of skin colors, are completely bound up—shackled—by America's original sin.

That wasn't the end of Whitney's store of suffering and sor-row. At the far end of the property, there were two sacred memorials. First, I came to the Field of Angels, which memo-rialized the brief lives of over twenty-two hundred infants who had died in slavery in Louisiana before reaching their third birthdays. In the whisper of a breeze, I could sense a deep, keening anguish that rustled the trees around me. It was weighted with the unassuageable grief of the mothers whose babies had died without ever breathing freedom or tasting security. Though stunned at the immensity of the grief, I fol-lowed the docent's directions to find on the surrounding wall a child who shared my birthday or name. I located the names of two infants who, like me, were born in early May. I paused for a moment on the tree-shaded benches next to other visitors, overcome with heartbreak and unspeakable sorrow. Within the encircling walls, on the simple center platform, a bronze angel gently cradled a small child, tenderly gazing into its still face. The loss of life and loss of hope recollected here were beyond comprehension.

Then I tiptoed to the Wall of Honor across the lane. Reading the dark granite walls etched with hundreds of individual names added bone-deep shame to my somber recollections. The engravings simply recorded people's places of origin, birthdates (if known), occupations, and ages at the time of their deaths. The docent instructed us to read the names aloud: "Say their names." I did, and I also sampled the short quotes and vignettes recorded on the wall, details taken from the oral history project. One woman's life became etched in my memory. She said: "I hate that man with every fiber of my being. How could he sell his own daughter into slavery? He stole my mother from me!" Her meaning dawned on me, and I was revolted: the man was her grandfather, her father, and her owner. He was her mother's rapist, and the heartless brute who had separated the daughter and her mother from each other. I thought of Barbara Holmes's description of the captives' moans: the sound "would break the heart of all who heard it."[11]

I continued slowly down the avenues, whispering the names of as many individuals as I could to honor their humanity. In the grave silence, under the crystal sunshine, the monuments cried out: "*Shema!* Pay attention! Do something!"

Before visiting Whitney, I had been able to distance myself from the horror of plantation labor by picturing the victims according to their enslaved status or people caught in a tragic system that had been consigned to history. However, Whitney's spruced-up green grounds and tranquility could not mask the

---

[11] Holmes, *Joy Unspeakable*, 50.

unfathomable suffering and brutality that the plantation's sun-drenched cane fields had witnessed. The sacred ground now cradled the bones and blood of human beings worked to death to produce wealth for the people who enslaved them. Later, Black sharecroppers produced crops for white-owned factories and anyone else in the sugar production process, from field to table, who stole their labor. The crimes in this small pocket of Louisiana multiplied by the millions of human beings enslaved in this country and across the American continents stunned my spirit. Now, I could not "unsee" what I had seen.

I completed writing about these recollections of America's original sin on display at Whitney during Holy Week in spring 2021. The horror and heartbreak that enveloped me in the cane fields of Louisiana merged into Good Friday's dirge: "Were you there when they crucified my Lord?" In this moment, there was no looking away.

Moment 4: Raising Cain

From the Louisiana cane fields, I traveled next to the Woodland Plantation "Cain-raising" of 1811. The play of words *cane* and *Cain* was irresistible for me, but captives' rebellions were deadly serious. Coined in nineteenth-century America, "raising Cain" described any unruliness and rioting that challenged the public order. To raise Cain was to cause trouble, to conjure the devil from hell, or to raise hell. In Genesis, Adam and Eve's son Cain killed his brother Abel in a fit of jealousy. In the New Testament, the civil and religious authorities crucified Jesus for rebelling against the status quo. Christ's resurrection continues to be the Cain-raising, world-disrupting event central to the meaning of Christianity. In this moment, I thought mostly about Christ's rebellious ministry, which was good trouble meant to instigate God's order of justice. Christ's ministry was the kind of turbulent but good trouble that Congressman John

Lewis counseled.[12] The 1811 German Coast Rebellion was the good, disruptive trouble that men and women captured on plantations raised to secure justice. It was also deadly serious trouble.

In this "raising Cain" moment, I pondered the skipped-over story of Black people enslaved on a Louisiana plantation who, in 1811, fought to the death for their freedom and for the emancipation of their fellow captives. Not infrequently, individuals escaped from plantation captivity. They took refuge in the swamps at the back edges of the fields. Colonies of escaped men and women, named *maroons*, from the French word for "untamable," lived in constant danger on the run. Snakes and animals just as much as slave catchers threatened their lives. The Code Noir punished escapees with branding for the first offense and maiming or death for repeat offenses.[13] Enslaved laborers caught congregating together or possessing weapons were branded, whipped, hobbled, or executed. Free Blacks as well as whites faced fines, enslavement, or imprisonment for assisting Black fugitives. Some rebels heroically made their way to free states in the North or to Canada to avoid recapture. The Fugitive Slave Law was one of many legal and extralegal techniques this nation used to suppress revolts and escapes, for it meant individuals who escaped from captivity were not safe from recapture anywhere in the United States.

[12] Representative John Lewis's statement on March 1, 2020, on the Edmund Pettus Bridge in Selma, Alabama, commemorating Bloody Sunday of 1965 has been widely referenced in academic and popular discussions: "Get in good trouble, necessary trouble, and redeem the soul of America." Rashawn Ray, "Five Things John Lewis Taught Us about Getting in 'Good Trouble,'" July 23, 2020, https://www.brookings.edu/blog/how-we-rise/2020/07/23/five-things-john-lewis-taught-us-about-getting-in-good-trouble/.

[13] Cyprian Davis and Jamie Phelps, eds., "Stamped with the Image of God," in *African Americans as God's Image in Black* (Maryknoll, NY: Orbis Books, 2003), 6–12.

The 1811 uprising was one of the most significant rebellions before the Civil War. I located the fading marker commemorating the Woodland Plantation "Cain-raising" beside West Airline Highway in Laplace, Louisiana. It was hidden behind traffic stanchions, utility poles, billboards, microwave towers, shimmering asphalt, and endless streams of cars.[14] Its obscure location symbolized for me how white America too often neglects to commemorate Black heroes who fought for their own emancipation against the tyranny of chattel slavery.

The 1811 battles occurred during a few days in early January. Mixed-race Afro-Haitian Charles Deslondes was singled out as the instigator of the rebellion, mostly discovered through the tortured confessions of other participants. Deslondes was a slave driver on the Andry family plantation, not far from Whitney. Only a few facts have been confirmed for certain, while there has been a great deal of historical speculation filling in the uprising's details. One cold night, several hundred domestic and field laborers slipped away into hush-darkened woods and gullies adjacent to the cane fields. They armed themselves with the only available weapons: sharp or heavy farm tools, sticks, and rocks. The fugitives' strategy was to kill the families who imprisoned them, burn buildings, set fire to fields, and free other captives along a downriver march to New Orleans. They hoped their numbers and decisive actions would forestall government troops just long enough to free all of the enslaved people in the region. Unfortunately, swiftly spreading news of the rebellion prompted the United States Army to march north along the river, routing the uprising in a few short days. The army rounded up at least 130 rebels. Deslondes and dozens of other leaders were convicted as instigators, gruesomely tortured, and then executed. The army impaled their

[14] Courtney Short and Clio Admin, "Historical Marker for the Location of the German Coast Slave Revolt of 1811," *Clio: Your Guide to History*, December 10, 2017, accessed January 26, 2021, https://theclio.com/entry/46715.

heads and left them to rot on spikes along the River Road. This routine vengeance both punished perpetrators and terrorized others who might have fought for freedom.[15]

I remembered that the Whitney Plantation, just down the way, had memorialized the Black rebels in a small parcel of ground at the edge of the property. In my recollection, I linked the ceramic installation of fifty-five Black men's heads impaled on silver spikes with the *Raise Up* sculpture by Hank Willis Thomas at the National Memorial for Peace and Justice (which I would visit in Montgomery in the week ahead). The lifelike visages of the heroes stopped me in my tracks, with realistic details of blood and anguish alive again. This was what American justice had looked like two hundred years ago: Black people slaughtered and displayed as a warning when they fought for the freedoms their nation had promised them.

It chilled me to the bone and threatened me, even across the centuries, to think of how the rebellion was squelched. The army's retribution upon the Black freedom fighters was nothing less than lynching. Terror and intimidation were the cruel goals of domination through agonizing violence. Lynching, even by military and law enforcement officers, even in times so different from contemporary moral sensibilities, violated basic principles of human decency. The governmental authorities

---

[15] Another rebellion rarely mentioned is the successful Haitian revolution from 1791 to 1804, which established Haiti as the first Black democracy in the world. The enslaved descendants of Africans won their freedom from France, one of the greatest military powers of the era, but Haitians have been paying a dear price for freedom for two hundred years. In the aftermath of the Haitian war for democracy, white-led nations, including the United States and Europe nations, embargoed Haiti; France demanded reparations for the land and labor the rebels had reclaimed; and the new democracy endured deep civil unrest for a long time afterward. Within the U.S., "Remember Haiti!" was a cautionary tale and a white rallying cry to crush all Black expressions of independence fiercely and decisively. The international response to Haitian independence to this day has been an economic and political lynching that punishes proud Haitians and denies the nation full partnership on the global stage. See, generally, Proenza-Coles, *American Founders*, 115–19.

chose torture, beheading, and public displays of the defeated rebels precisely to intimidate other captives. By executing victims in the most brutal way possible, they obliterated any lingering resistance harbored in onlookers' hearts. Domination through raw and violent power has been routinely used to enforce the color line and the racial caste system at the foundation of American society. Lynching has taken many forms, but it has always sought to destroy the prophets of justice, prophets by their words and deeds. I was staggered thinking that the response of our "equal justice for all" Christian nation and culture has been to lynch the justice seekers rather than to punish their enslavers.

So, taking a lesson from the Whitney docent, I have tried to shift my language in order to shift my understanding. The German Coast dissidents challenged state-sanctioned captivity as a fundamental denial of their freedom. Deslondes was a patriot. He gathered freedom fighters who sacrificed their lives to defeat the worst tyranny of their times. They took heroic measures to defend their lives and their families' well-being. Just like the 1776 patriots, the German Coast fighters were pro-democracy protesters, dissidents who challenged governmental oppression. The fact that they lost the 1811 battle for emancipation did not diminish their heroism. The battle was just one moment in a long but successful war—the Civil War— that abolished slavery. Like the founders who signed the Declaration of Independence, the 1811 revolutionaries fought for liberty and justice for all. Two hundred years after Deslondes's heroism, I recognized the German Coast rebellion as a prophetic "Cain-raising" moment of justice on the move.

As I turned back to New Orleans, I made one more inspired connection. I retold the 1811 story in terms of Jesus—a salvation-focused "God is with us" story. The surreptitious encounters and whispers of 1811 were like the Jewish peasants in Palestine wondering if Jesus of Nazareth was God's Messiah. The brace of individuals joining the rebellion's downriver march toward New Orleans reenacted Jesus' triumphant entry into Jerusalem. Deslondes's followers betrayed him to save themselves like Judas betrayed Jesus for thirty pieces of silver. Deslondes and Jesus both suffered vicious floggings and then bloodthirsty public mockery as they were strung up. They both died excruciating deaths as scapegoats and object lessons. They were both lynched, crucified because they stood against the status quo. Casting Deslondes in Jesus' role led me to an inescapable truth: Jesus is God among the outcasts. In his crucifixion, we see what justice will cost.

Certainly, this rebel moment along the Mississippi "raised Cain" for me and threatened to unshackle my too-safe faith. I heard God's fierce call renewed: "*Shema!* Walk with me a little further."

Moment 5: New Orleans Saints

Returning to New Orleans from the upriver rebellion moments, I wanted to sample Catholics' connections to slavery in this complicated Creole city. I grabbed my weathered black shillelagh and strode back to New Orleans to explore its Catholic origins, its saints, and its faithful Black believers.

Based on Louisiana's French lineage, I wasn't surprised that New Orleans's Catholic heritage was everywhere. As I found in earlier French Quarter moments, saints' names marked the streets, and churches adorned every other corner. The city boasted a litany of hometown holy women and men: St. Frances Xavier Cabrini, St. Katharine Drexel, St. Rose Philippine Duchesne, Blessed Francis Xavier Seelos, Venerable Henriette Delille, Venerable Cornelia Connelly, Mother Margaret Haughery. As I prayed the saints' names, I recalled my five-year-old daughter asking me, years ago, from the back seat of the car: "How do you get to be a saint?" I told her that saints love God and love other people. The two great commandments that God has enjoined upon us were simple enough for a child to grasp. Love God and neighbor. "OK!" she vowed. Everything seemed possible, even easy, in her not-yet-tainted innocence.

Tragically, the Roman Catholic Church, with all its holy men and women saints, was a major catalyst for the intertwined disasters of global exploration and chattel slavery at the end of the Middle Ages. Its principal error, in my mind, was the fateful "doctrine of discovery." Popes declared that lands not inhabited by Christians were available to be discovered by European Catholics and occupied. The non-Christian inhabitants could be consigned to perpetual slavery and baptized— for their own good. This launched a race for conquest and cultural exploitation under the veil of a holy crusade.[16] European nations claimed rights over most of the land in the American continents, although their style of conquest and colonization varied. The common tragedy was that, at every

---

[16] A series of fifteenth-century papal proclamations launched a wave of plunder rooted in the "doctrine of discovery." The three most relevant papal bulls are *Dum Diversas*, 1452; *Romanus Pontifex*, 1454; and *Inter Caetera*, 1493. See Vinne Rotondaro, "Disastrous Doctrine Had Papal Roots," *National Catholic Reporter Online*, September 4, 2015, https://www.ncronline.org /news/justice/disastrous-doctrine-had-papal-roots. The rights of white Europeans included the privilege to take the lives, labor, and lands of other human beings. Portuguese, French, and Spanish adventurers with papal authority and royal treaties colonized Caribbean islands, the Gulf shores, and South American jungles. French explorers settled New Orleans at the mouth of the Mississippi under the auspices of their monarch. King Louis XV promulgated the Code Noir of 1724 to govern the legal rights between whites and Blacks in French plantation colonies, which included the Louisiana Territory. The Code reserved land ownership for Catholics and required enslavers to baptize and catechize the men and women whom they forced to work on the plantations. By 1839, in *Supremo Apostolos*, Pope Gregory XVI repudiated prior papal pronouncements and denounced slave trading as a "shame" upon Christian nations, as "absolutely unworthy of the Christian name." Defying Pope Gregory, Catholic religious orders and Catholic individuals continued to own slaves in the United States until the Emancipation Proclamation in 1863. Thus, the Catholic Church in this country approved enslavement of Africans for labor, under the protection of the Vatican. Even the pope could not control the demon of greed and European supremacy that had been unleashed. See also John Francis Maxwell, *Slavery and the Catholic Church: The History of Catholic Teaching Concerning the Moral Legitimacy of the Institution of Slavery* (London: Barry Rose Publishers, 1975).

turn, they brutally disregarded the humanity of the indigenous inhabitants.

New Orleans's distinctive expression of Catholicism stemmed from its situation as a slave port and a French colony governed by the 1724 Code Noir on the frontier of an otherwise Protestant-majority America.[17] Far from the British Protestant influence on the Eastern Seaboard, New Orleans Catholics absorbed many of the cultural influences of African indigenous traditions. Congo Square markets and Sunday minglings brought more recently arrived Africans into regular contact with established residents of color, many of whom were already Catholic. They incorporated ring circles and call-and-response into Catholic liturgies. African cosmologies and ancestor worship also linked up within the Catholic saint-filled heavens and Mother of God venerations. Mardi Gras radiated with a sensuous abandonment to music, food, and dance—clearly not a product of guilt-inflected Baltimore Catholic influences. In a virtuous cycle, the assimilation of African traditions into New Orleans's Catholicism facilitated the evangelization of newcomers into communities that already reflected their presence.

While racial divisions were not erased, many opportunities existed for relationships across color lines in this city in the nineteenth century. Several factors contributed to this. Well into that period, French priests were assigned to New Orleans parishes; they were less acculturated to chattel slavery than American clergy. A number of religious congregations professed specific charisms to serve African Americans, enslaved or free. There were the Josephite priests (the Society of St. Joseph, originating in Mill Hill, England, and then moving to Baltimore upon its American founding) and a women's order, the Society

---

[17] An 1858 letter by the Bishop of Natchez, William Henry Elder, noted that approximately half of the population of the New Orleans diocese was enslaved but there were too few priests to offer them sacraments. Davis and Phelps, *Stamped with the Image of God*, 32–35.

of the Sacred Heart, founded in France and transported to Mississippi by St. Rose Philippine Duchesne in the 1800s. St. Katherine Drexel, a member of the Congregation of the Blessed Sacrament from a wealthy Philadelphia family, spent her personal fortune in Louisiana to educate Africans and their descendants, and Native Americans. Without directly repudiating chattel slavery, Catholics of all races worshipped in the same church buildings because of the Catholic commitment to a universal church, pledged as one to the Bishop of Rome.

Enslaved African women especially dominated parish life in New Orleans in this era. African men and women, severed from homelands and traditions, following sankofa wisdom, rebuilt strong personal ties in the new land by transplanting deep-rooted social and tribal customs. These customs often accorded African women profound respect and authority not available to white women. To replace lost community and kinship, African women adopted the role of godmother to shepherd newcomers into parish communities, which in turn reinforced spiritual and religious bonds. Additionally, the church's social and political sway in Catholic New Orleans enabled Black women, free and enslaved, to improve their own and their children's lives in tangible ways. All of these factors in the racially restricted society of antebellum Louisiana fostered in women of color a potent blend of autonomy and religious authority.

Free Black Catholic women left their mark upon New Orleans, as I learned when I encountered Venerable Henriette Delille.[18] For me, her deeds spoke more persuasively than any writings she left behind because of the way she defied cultural norms. As a fair-skinned woman of color, Henriette Delille was born legally free, but her freedom was wholly circumscribed by

---

[18] For background on Venerable Henriette Delille, see M. Shawn Copeland, *The Subversive Power of Love: The Vision of Henriette Delille* (Mahwah, NJ: Paulist Press, 2009).

white men in the white-dominated culture. Society expected her to become a concubine to a white man, possibly with some limited power to negotiate for her children's freedom and easier movement through the city. Instead, she followed an early call into vowed religious life. In 1842, with two friends, she founded the Sisters of the Holy Family, a congregation for women of color (segregated by law). I located a yellowing photograph of Mother Henriette in which she appeared austerely dressed, without ornaments or color. Peering beyond her formidable bearing, my gaze settled upon her gentle face and soft eyes. Calm and sure. Resolute in her purpose. Over a number of decades, Mother Henriette and her sisters overcame numerous legal, financial, and cultural constraints to establish a religious order and a school for the children of enslaved residents of New Orleans. They also established a hospice for residents of color, free or enslaved. Despite the ravages of time and hurricanes, St. Mary's Academy and the Lafon Nursing Facility continue to serve people of color in New Orleans to this day. Love God and love your neighbor.

As I walked with Mother Henriette in this moment, I tried to embrace the meaning of her witness. This saint-in-waiting had summoned the Catholic Church in her time to protect the human dignity of people of color, to live up to its convictions that all people are the children of God. The schools and hospital that she established demonstrated what securing human dignity looks like. Her work was a signpost for those of us who would follow her. Despite the stark contrast between Deslondes and Mother Henriette Delille, I realized that both of them had been insurgents. I recognized a "God is with us" witness in their heroic and defiant sacrifices to emancipate others from the unjust burdens of life imposed upon them by law and custom. Both saints pointed to essential qualities of Jesus Christ: Christ as prophetic disrupter and Christ as tender healer. Deslondes and Mother Henriette enfleshed Jesus' fierce love and sacrifice for justice.

Young Ruby Bridges was one of the children who had integrated the all-white William Frantz Elementary School in Orleans Parish. Norman Rockwell's well-known painting *The Problem We All Live With* depicts her walking in, head held high, with U.S. Marshals surrounding her. She prayed for her persecutors as she moved her feet: "Please God, try to forgive those people. Because even if they say those bad things, they don't know what they're doing. So You could forgive them, just like You did those folks a long time ago when they said terrible things about You."

Ruby Bridges's Prayer[19]

After witnessing the struggles of New Orleans's rebels and saints, I reclaimed the gold necklace that my husband had given me nearly thirty years ago. A small representation of Christ crucified hung from the chain. For a decade or more, I was unsure whether the necklace was merely jewelry for me or whether it made a statement of faith. In this saints' moment, I discerned a new direction: the crucified Christ signified a trinity of intertwined truths—our sin, God's mercy, and our path to life. It meant that I could not delay encountering God until I crossed death's boundary into a heaven-promised future. The cross-suspended Jesus summoned me to meet God in all-too-common crucifixion moments. I reclaimed Christ on the cross by clasping the necklace on again. It would remain tucked beneath my shirt collar against my skin as a talisman from this race and grace pilgrimage to remind me—moment by moment—to seek God with and among my neighbors.

I had more stops to make in New Orleans, more signposts to meet. Walk with me and *Shema!*

---

[19] Flora Wilson Bridges describes the courage of Ruby Bridges in attending an all-white elementary school and publishes her prayer in *Resurrection Song: African-American Spirituality* (New York: Orbis Press, 2001), 104–5 (citations omitted).

Moment 6: Black and Catholic[20]

In this Black and Catholic moment, I made my way back to present-day New Orleans for a Sunday morning Mass at Blessed Sacrament - St. Joan of Arc Parish, a mixed but mostly African American community. The church was one hundred years young and thrumming with the life of the Spirit. Like everything else in New Orleans—really, in the United States—past enslavement and segregation explained the present moment of this African American parish. Around the turn of the twentieth century, the Archdiocese of New Orleans faced a double challenge: absorbing the influx of European immigrants and addressing the sacramental needs of newly freed field and household laborers. Wrapped in fears about miscegenation and threats to social equality, the archbishop strictly segregated formerly mixed-race parishes. When the parish of Mater Dolorosa built a new church on Carrollton Avenue for its growing membership, all parishioners regardless of their racial or immigration status contributed money and time to the building. Just as the doors were to open for worship in 1914, the archbishop ordered all Black parishioners to remain behind in the old sanctuary. Despite the parish's abandonment, Black families have remained a Catholic anchor of the neighborhood for over a century. In a similar Jim Crow blow, Blessed Sacrament parish, located a few miles north of St. Joan of Arc, was also forcibly segregated under the pretense that segregation served the people's interests. Blessed Sacrament and St. Joan of Arc merged in 2009 into a single parish and school community still served by the Josephite Fathers. Black has meant in Catholic New Orleans that a person nevertheless was not

---

[20] This phrase is the title of an important collection of essays about African American contributions in the Catholic Church in this country and to Catholic theology more generally. See Jamie T. Phelps, ed., *Black and Catholic: The Challenge and Gift of Black Folk; Contributions of African American Experience and Thought to Catholic Theology* (Milwaukee, WI: Marquette University Press, 1997).

really, not fully, a child of God and a sister or brother in Christ. Things have been changing, but the promised land of God's covenanted community of racial justice remains a not-yet reality for this archdiocese and for the American Catholic Church as a whole.

Under scudding clouds on my October visit, the neighborhood's mood was bright and easy. Outside the church, I took a few minutes to study the inspiring bronze relief above the main entrance that portrayed St. Joan of Arc brandishing a ribbon-decorated cross. Just like the young woman warrior who dared to challenge the king in her day, the imposing facade defied the Mississippi's mighty waters, held back behind the looming levees a few hundred yards away. Inside the church, a friendly hubbub embraced me under the brown-trussed ceiling. The simple, uncluttered space invited me to relax as early arrivers mingled, sharing news of families and friends. Individual members greeted me since it was clear to anyone that I was a stranger to the church and the region. I was grateful to be included in their warm smiles and to be welcomed in the house of God. I couldn't miss the worshippers who adorned themselves in the black and gold of the New Orleans Saints in anticipation of the game that afternoon. I wasn't familiar with a lot of the music, but its contagious joy enveloped me all the same.

During Mass, I considered how comfortable I felt at Blessed Sacrament - St. Joan of Arc. Certainly it had to do with the community's gracious warmth, but it also derived from the style of Black Catholic worship, which I have experienced at my home parish—St. Columba in Oakland, California. Before the COVID quarantine that began in March 2020, I went regularly to Mass and parish celebrations at St. Columba during the academic year. St. Columba's banners and social media streams announced that the community worshipped "in the African American tradition." This has meant plenty of singing that includes spirituals and protest hymns, plenty of religious symbols that reflect the look and culture of the community, and plenty of hugs at the doors and throughout Mass. The sign of peace was not over until everyone had hugged everyone else. Call-and-response was expected during homilies when preachers, lay and ordained, warmed and rallied to calls of encouragement from the pews. Nearly every Sunday, the sermons-on-fire would address contemporary social issues, linking our human needs to Jesus and the Old Testament prophets. The parish family drew its touchstone joy from the expression printed on the Sunday bulletins: "We know who and whose we are."[21]

I connected the Blessed Sacrament-St. Joan of Arc welcome with my first visits to St. Columba, when I found unanticipated acceptance all around. The parish custom was for new attendees to introduce themselves at the end of Mass. On my first weekend there, I shared that I worked for the Jesuit School of Theology, so the community promised not to hold the Jesuit connections against me. On my second weekend, I introduced my husband, who had joined me. As I was saying his name, the pastor cautioned: "We let people speak for themselves at St. Columba." After some embarrassed confusion, I was able to laugh with everyone else. But the lesson of inclusion has not left me—people speak for themselves!

But St. Columba had another claim to fame. When a friend of mine recounted to me her first visit to the parish and the same welcome she had felt, she concluded, "And I have seen God at St. Columba. She sits at the side entrance to the church, majestic and matronly in her kente cloth finery." I knew immediately the person she spoke about: a regal African American woman who sat by the sanctuary door. Every Sunday morning, through several Masses, she sat in the backmost pew, greeting and directing the ebb and flow of the worshippers. Regardless of a person's posture or presentation, regardless of whose hands they held or how they dressed, God greeted the St. Columba

---

[21] St. Columba Parish Bulletins, accessed August 27, 2021, https://stcolumba -oak.com/bulletins.

family at the door of the sanctuary. God was enfleshed in a Black woman's graciously extended arms.

I realized that I should have been attending to the homily at Blessed Sacrament-St. Joan of Arc but my heart in that moment was filled with gratitude for the parish family of St. Columba who had accepted me among their members. Through their relentless, fierce, and faithful witness, I have learned something about being catholic—with a small "c," meaning universal. To be catholic means to include everyone. The parishioners of St. Columba have been signposts of catholic love, catholic justice, and a catholic welcome table.

After Sunday Mass, it was time to finish up my color-line trek in New Orleans. Hurricane Katrina had upended life in this city fifteen years ago, and the scars remained raw and visible. I had to see them for myself. Walk with me. *Shema!*

Moment 7: The Lower Ninth Ward

The Lower Ninth Ward was not far from the parish of Blessed Sacrament-St. Joan of Arc, but it was hard to find because of the city's complicated network of canals and bridges. I had second thoughts about the prospect of touring the struggling neighborhood, feeling like a "poverty gawker." My trepidation reminded me not to use my white-value frames as the lens for the moment. I recalled a similar trenchant admonishment voiced by Henry Louis Gates Jr. Narrating a video documentary on Haiti, he cautioned that poverty was not the Haitian identity. The nation's identity was its African heritage, its citizens' spiritual depth, and their creative power.[22] That resonated with

---

[22] Henry Louis Gates Jr., "Haiti and the Dominican Republic: An Island Divided," *Black in Latin America*, PBS, https://www.pbs.org/wnet/black-in -latin-america/featured/haiti-the-dominican-republic-an-island-divided -watch-full-episode/165/; Marvin Earl Lawson, "Black in Latin America Haiti and the Dominican Republic," reposted March 2, 2016, video, 51:25, accessed March 15, 2021, https://www.youtube.com/watch?v=DD4A9UET5TI&t =2472s.

the Whitney docent's practice of rejecting the easy label of "slave," which reduced the individuals held captive on the land to a single dimension, once more stealing the fullness of their lives from them. *Shema!* I reminded myself to open my mind and heart to the residents of New Orleans's Lower Ninth Ward on their own terms in their own neighborhood. They speak for themselves.

I visited the neighborhood late on a Sunday afternoon with several companions. Just a few miles east of the French Quarter, the Lower Ninth's stillness contrasted with the distant *shush* of highway traffic just beyond our sight. A gray overcast sky hung low above us, threatening heavy raindrops. The sky's menace competed with the imposing, not-wholly-to-be-trusted levees on the neighborhood's south and west edges. We wandered along the sunken crisscrossing of streets not yet repaired since Hurricane Katrina hit in 2005. Garbage was piled up on some plots, like unregulated dumps, surely attracting rats and other rodent vermin. Weed-infested lots with crumbling foundations and their front stoops to nowhere bordered other yards that hosted glass-clad modern homes and cheerful pastel cottages. We dodged fire ants in the tall grasses and watched warily for snakes. The ward was clearly depopulated, with perhaps one in four or five houses obviously still uninhabitable. Under the leaden sky, the chill of one thousand lost lives hushed us into a sacred silence, as if we had stepped into a churchyard or walked upon holy ground.

The city of New Orleans annexed the sugar-growing land on its eastern flank in 1852, now designated as the Lower Ninth Ward. The label "Lower" pinpointed the area's location—further down the river from the French Quarter, closer to the Delta and the Gulf. The Holy Cross neighborhood was also lower in elevation compared to the city proper; its northernmost streets were below sea level. The 1920s construction of the Industrial Canal, which ran southward from Lake Pontchartrain to the Mississippi River, isolated the neighborhood from the thriving commerce of the Port of New Orleans. By the 1950s, only about half of the land in the Lower Ninth Ward had been developed. The neighborhood had long been home to a mostly Black population and has been among the poorest districts in New Orleans, which is the poorest city in Louisiana, which is the poorest state in the United States.[23] At the time of the Katrina disaster, Lower Ninth Ward residents were twice as likely to need food stamps, earned approximately half as much income as the average New Orleans residents, and were poorer than residents in nearby census tracts. No matter what we tell ourselves about the American Dream, poverty predicts a person's life chances, health outcomes, educational access, and likelihood of incarceration.

"On block after block, entire houses had been swept off their foundations, with corner stores and other businesses flattened. Splintered trees. Dirty, rusting cars scattered at odd angles. More than a thousand dead. What remained was a shallow layer of muck, canal water and sewage as far as the eye could see. Mold began to devour everything on the inside. And eventually this northern part of the Lower 9 became the largest demolition of a community in modern U.S. history as whole neighborhoods were bulldozed away. It is estimated that of 220 square blocks from Claiborne Avenue to the Bayou, only 140 homes were left—most of those uninhabitable."

Lower Ninth Ward Center for Sustainable Development[24]

Most American adults have vivid memories of Hurricane Katrina in late August 2005, when the storm flooded and then drowned New Orleans. Savage stormy images swamped our

---

[23] See United States Census Bureau, "Zip Code 70117," *United States Zip Codes.org*, 2021, accessed February 15, 2021, https://www.unitedstateszip codes.org/70117/#stats.

[24] "Hurricanes Katrina and Rita," *Lower Ninth Ward Center for Sustainable Development*, 2020, http://sustainthenine.org/hurricanes-katrina-rita/.

smart phones and TVs. The levees could not sustain the extraordinary assault of wind and water. The water ripped into the Lower Ninth Ward, inundating it with roof-high waves.[25] Neighborhood residents and civic leaders were not surprised that the levees failed. Repeated calls from private and municipal organizations to the national government to reengineer the levee system had been ignored. It was too expensive for taxpayers to protect vulnerable human beings in a low-income neighborhood. When the rain-swollen river breached its levees, storm-surging waters avalanched down the soil flanks of the Industrial Canal. The flood waters, emancipated from narrowed channels, washed away lives and livelihoods in the ward. Reporting on life in New Orleans after the levees broke, news media broadcasted photos of "looters" who were Black and "flood victims" who were not, all of whom were trying to salvage food and water after the nation had abandoned them to the storm.[26]

Katrina had destroyed or damaged 100 percent of the homes in the Lower Ninth Ward. All of the dwellings were flooded. Of 4,800 households in 2005, about 37 percent were rebuilt and inhabited 15 years later.[27] The expression "a comedy of errors" came to my mind, but that would have made a mockery of the injustice. The Lower Ninth Ward was rather "a tragedy of indifference." Federal and local agencies' indifference to the vulnerability of communities of color compounded the Cate-

[25] See, e.g., Debbie Elliot, "Lower Ninth Ward Residents Remember When the Levees Failed New Orleans," NPR, August 25, 2005, www.npr.org /2015/08/25/434513743/lower-ninth-ward-residents-remember-when-the -levees-failed-new-orleans.

[26] See, e.g., "Katrina Coverage Exposes Race, Class Fault Lines," RACE from NPR, September 13, 2005, ttps://www.npr.org/templates/story/story .php?storyId=4844457.

[27] Greg Allen, "Ghosts of Katrina Still Haunt New Orleans' Shattered Lower Ninth Ward," Special Series, August 3, 2015, https://www.npr.org/2015/08 /03/427844717/ghosts-of-katrina-still-haunt-new-orleans-shattered-lower -ninth-ward.

gory Five hurricane's destructive power. Even FEMA's relief efforts exacerbated the devastation. The trailers for temporary shelter were laced with carcinogenic formaldehyde because the imported drywall was substandard. Homeowners' housing reimbursements were tied to outdated purchase prices rather than to the cost of rebuilding; few residents could afford to return even years later. The city delayed and then refused to fix roads, sewers, and lighting in the ward because of declining population and low tax revenues. All of this was predictable and avoidable.

As I paced through the Lower Ninth Ward on that fall afternoon, I was haunted by the anguish of Katrina refugees whose lives had been washed away in a matter of moments. Denise Bennett recounted how she and her family shivered through a night of rain on a rooftop in St. Bernard Parish, not far from the Lower Ninth. They waited twelve hours for rescue, afraid they would be swept away in the swirling waters around their feet.[28] Her feelings of gut-wrenching abandonment and despair rang out in the sheer terror of her retelling. Many storm refugees were literally confined in the Superdome and the Ernest N. Morial Convention Center. The media had been broadcasting exaggerated and sensational stories of rape and pillage in New Orleans. In fact, the hurricane survivors had been trying desperately to help each other, sharing what food and water they could find, frantic to attract relief from the outside world. They urgently needed food, medical care, and even basic hygiene such as functioning toilets. One reporter described the atrocious, desperate scene at the convention center, lawlessness, people condemned to be "living like animals."[29] "The rules of society" no longer applied, but no one was coming to help. Black New Orleans residents had been abandoned by their

---

[28] "Hurricane Katrina: 10 Years of Recovery and Reflection," Special Series, August 29, 2015, https://www.npr.org/series/429056277/hurricane-katrina -10-years-of-recovery-and-reflection.
[29] "Hurricane Katrina."

fellow citizens, once again. In the words of an African American spiritual, "Sometimes I feel like a motherless child."

Stories like these ought to move us, I thought. The brutal captivity of laborers on river plantations had moved Deslondes; Catholic saints and servants had responded compassionately to the cries of New Orleans's outcasts for centuries. Their actions highlighted for me the difference between pity and justice. After the fact, suffering moves us to pity and rescue. However, justice is anticipatory. The work of justice is to create the conditions for thriving neighbors and a flourishing community grounded in human dignity and interpersonal relationships. More precisely, I realized that the flooding destruction of the Lower Ninth Ward was a predictable result of American public policy. By our choices, our nation accounts some lives more important than others. The Lower Ninth Ward displayed this truth.

The Lower Ninth Ward also revealed the residents' resilience and the power of people who struggle for justice for themselves and their communities. Several nonprofits have been active in this district since Hurricane Katrina hit. Among the ward's cracked foundations and abandoned stoops, new houses and new lives were taking shape. Nevertheless, neighborhood pride and hard work do not absolve this nation of its responsibility to address structural racism and the entrenched caste system. Racial justice does not mean retaining the flawed system. It cannot limit itself to extending charity and affirming words. A living commitment to racial justice means a renovated system where everyone can find a place at the table, where the path forward is built by and for all. The Lower Ninth Ward taught me this and more.[30]

In the fierce urgency of now, God was inviting me beyond recollection to conversion. To reckon with racism would mean facing my story within our nation's past decisions, acknowl-

---

[30] Another Category 4 hurricane (Ida) with 150-mile-per-hour winds made landfall on the Louisiana coast in late August 2021. This time the levees held.

edging the injustices, and beginning to repair them. Without meaning to be naive, I tentatively grasped this ray of hope. Original sin means more than being caught in the webbed legacy of past choices. Original sin is not inexorable destiny. Original sin is propensity, likelihood—but not fate. God's grace makes justice possible. As I realized that this nation is shackled by its past, bound to it, I also glimpsed the possibility of unshackling from the past.

Unshackling from the Past

In closing these moments of my pilgrimage in New Orleans, I gathered a harvest of memories from the past and present witnesses I had met. I recollected and sifted what I had learned. The *Miserere*, Psalm 51, accompanied me and offered me wisdom as I paused to glean graces from this week: "For I know my transgressions, / and my sin is always before me. . . . Yet you desired faithfulness even in the womb; / you taught me wisdom in that secret place" (vv. 3 and 6). The verses reminded me of how I learned to approach the sacrament of reconciliation as a child. Penance is its old-fashioned, guilt-inducing name. The path to reconciliation with God and our sisters and brothers begins with a clear-sighted acknowledgement of our sins. Then, acknowledgment has to be followed with a sincere effort to repair the harm we caused by rebalancing our personal and communal relationships for justice.

In the flash of this second week on pilgrimage, I could only begin to examine my conscience and our country's conscience about our racial sins. So many places and perspectives had to be gathered up and saved for later consideration. So many more voices had yet to be heard. Nevertheless, this pilgrimage excavated deeply disturbing layers of our nation's slaveholding self and revealed slavery's legacy as "always before me." As I experienced New Orleans, from the ship docks on the Mississippi where human beings were unloaded for sale, to the sugar plantations that had been locales of violence-forced labor, to the Lower Ninth Ward and its too-slow recovery, this nation's racial sins were—are—displayed in plain sight. Images of slave-binding shackles linked the harrowing moments of the week. Shackles cut deep into human wrists, ankles, and necks, girdling them in heavy iron that crushed hope. I had not wanted to know about the brutality that launched the United States' global empire. Because of this moment, I have started to listen more deeply to the humanity of the people in bondage in this nation, past and present. In doing so, I have tried to connect my own story to their lives and to find ties that bind us.

The moments of this week displayed for me long-standing wounds of injustice still unacknowledged and thus unhealed. With open eyes, attentive ears, and a softened heart, I recognized in this week the echoes of profound human suffering that reverberate today. For the suffering that I have tried not to see, for the injustice that our nation has tried to hide, may God open my eyes. May God teach me sincerity and wisdom. May God give me a heart that beats with compassion. May I *Shema!* May I hear the cries for justice and respond swiftly.

Then I wondered how I would find the wisdom and courage that I sought. How would I know what justice was unless I learned from the saints and signposts who have led the way? The third week on this race and grace pilgrimage paced me forward in time to Civil Rights moments in the justice reckoning that shook the nation during the 1950s and '60s. Walk with me to join the Deep South revolution.

Third Week
A Deep South Revolution

This third week on pilgrimage, I traveled a hundred years and a thousand miles from nineteenth-century New Orleans to the Deep South of the 1950s and '60s. During the second week, I had listened to voices of human beings rebelling against the captivity of racism in all its forms. I also found fierce saintly love that asserted human dignity and testified to hope amidst the weeds of the Lower Ninth Ward. Although slavery in the Confederate states had legally ended with the Emancipation Proclamation, oppression of African Americans continued, and white power developed new means of racial exploitation. The worst of these were Jim Crow segregation and publicly condoned lynchings that shackled African Americans into second-class citizenship. Then something remarkable happened in this country about sixty years ago because of the freedom marches led by Black civic leaders and pastors. In the region where slavery used to reign—the Deep South—a second American revolution was waged for the civil rights of all people in this country.

In a disturbing reminder of how far this country still needs to march, I completed these recollections on the day that a Minneapolis jury convicted Derek Chauvin of murdering George Floyd. White supremacy has not been vanquished, and an inclusive multiracial America is not yet a reality. Still, I wanted to meet the champions of the movement in moments of struggle to understand the long shadow of America's original sin. My quest led me from Montgomery to Selma and then to

Atlanta. I wanted to visit the celebrated sites so that I might
be transformed by the dawning promise days of the movement
that had fired my imagination for so long. I took up my shillelagh, my crucifix, my prayers, and my courage. I squared
my shoulders with a sacred wind at my back. With wide-open
eyes, I set my sights on Alabama and Georgia. I stepped into
the whirlwind of the Deep South revolution.

Moment 1: Strange Fruit

On a crisp, late fall morning, the grass shimmered with dew
under the warming Alabama sunshine. A few birds sang, but
an unbroken stillness swathed the Montgomery neighborhood
just a few blocks from where people had once been auctioned.
The group I traveled with that day gathered for prayer at the
gates of the National Memorial for Peace and Justice.

> "Southern trees bear a strange fruit,
> Blood on the leaves and blood at the root,
> Black body swinging in the Southern breeze,
> Strange fruit hanging from the poplar trees."
>
> Abel Meeropol, "Strange Fruit"[1]

Tall metal pikes set in concrete separated this sanctified
ground from the surrounding neighborhood. Surely we entered a liminal space, a place of "holy remembrance." Our
somber mood deepened as we listened to Billie Holiday's
haunting, heartrending performance of "Strange Fruit." Tears
streamed down some people's faces; shock stilled the breath

---

[1] "Strange Fruit" was composed by Abel Meeropol, but Billie Holiday's
voice is what most people recall about this disturbing protest song. Elizabeth
Blair, "The Strange Story of the Man Behind Strange Fruit," *Morning Edition*,
NPR, September 5, 2012, https://www.npr.org/2012/09/05/158933012
/the-strange-story-of-the-man-behind-strange-fruit.

of others. A couple of complete strangers joined in *communitas* with us on bended knees. We silently prayed in memory of lynching's infernal reign of terror during Jim Crow. The Equal Justice Initiative has documented the death of thousands of women and men, even children, nearly all African Americans, who were lynched in the United States of America after the Reconstruction's brief flowering of hope.

I entered the memorial compound through a short enclosed walkway, a foreboding doorway of no return. I was dumb-founded. Literally. Silence embraced my whole being. The memorial offered no talking exhibits to explain what visitors were supposed to learn. There was no music, no announce-ment, no chatter. Stillness weighted my chest and numbed my spirit. The mood was grave and anticipatory, as if we had gath-ered for a loved one's funeral. The only sounds were visitors' soft gasps and stifled sobs. Nothing distracted us from the martyrs' memories. In the arresting silence, I swear I heard sorrow crushing our hearts.

Two imposing bronze statue clusters framed the memorial experience, one at the entrance and one at the exit. They con-tinue to haunt my recollection. In the words of Psalm 51, which kept circling in my mind, "[M]y sin is ever before me" (v. 3). The first grouping, just inside the entrance gate, depicted a small band of individuals in postures from profound anguish to majestic resistance. All were Africans, barely clothed and without possessions. Oxidizing iron chains, now staining the figures' bodies with orange-red streaks, yoked their necks and feet together. Their shackles bound them into a disturbing community, a coffle, simultaneously isolated and joined. Their suffering set them apart and linked them.

Perhaps they represented a family, I thought as I interrogated one woman's face. With breasts exposed for anyone to see, she cradled an infant in the crook of her left arm. Her extended right hand nearly caressed a man's proud shoulder just barely out of reach. "May I touch my beloved one more time!" her expression seemed to say. Soon, very soon, they would be separated forever at the auction block. Three of the figures kneeled, a man and two women, with arms wrenched and chained behind their backs. Other visitors squatted before the figures, as did I, peering deeply into the suffering abyss of their eyes. I could not name what I saw in their bodies or their faces. If we could fathom their hearts, how would we bear the unspeakable torment of human beings bound away into chattel slavery? I realized that in our times, when we discuss the enslavement of human beings, we speak of its economic devastation and in general terms about the human cost. It seems too painful, too shameful, perhaps, to open our hearts intimately to slavery's human anguish.

The second statue cluster was poised above sloping lawns at the memorial's exit. The city skyline rose beyond the perimeter fence. Cement walkways crisscrossed the yard, offering granite benches where visitors could sit to consider the sculpture from all directions. Young trees promised shade in the years ahead, but for now their sparse branches reinforced the statute's stark lines. Shaped of bronze like the first grouping, this sculpture reenacted a more contemporary but still timeless terror. Atop a six-foot concrete wall, I saw a line of a dozen Black men's heads and shoulders framed by their upraised arms. "Hands up!" The men's frozen expressions radiated a mixture of palpable fear and defiance. This has been the imploring posture that powerless Black Americans, and indeed all people of color, have adopted before law enforcement officers, hoping they would not be killed for living. But raising their hands has too often failed to protect them from indifference to their humanity. The lynching time in our nation has not yet ended. In 2020, 22 percent of the 999 people whom law officers shot and killed in the U.S. were African Americans, even though this demographic comprises only about 13 percent of the nation's population.[2] More importantly, these statistics refer to human beings: loved ones with names, families, and

---

[2] "Number of People Shot to Death by the Police in the United States from 2017 to 2021 by Race," *Statistica*, accessed April 10, 2021, https://www.statista.com/statistics/585152/people-shot-to-death-by-us-police-by-race/.

lost futures. As I wrote this moment recollecting the National Peace and Justice Memorial, news media reported on the deaths of Ma'Khia Bryant, Daunte Wright, Adam Toledo, Ronald Greene, and Andrew Brown Jr. at the hands of police. The culminating tableau in the memorial cemented the connection between past lynchings and present white caste power bent on extinguishing Black and brown lives.

Bookended by the entrance and exit statues, the memorial's centerpiece was a casket-shrouded labyrinth. Metal coffins, eight hundred in total, were suspeneded from the roof. I walked through the steel boxes, first passing markers at shoulder height and then moving beneath them when the concrete slanted downward. They signposted the counties in the U.S. where one or more persons had been lynched since the Civil War. Lynching happened throughout the nation, not just in the South. As I paced, I felt the witness and weight of human violence, inconceivable in its magnitude. Aghast, I read individual names—one, two, or even five people may have shared the same surname. Families were murdered together on a single day, I realized, in a perverse festival of white-mob holiday-making. Treading carefully along the concrete ramp, I read the death-worthy offenses etched upon the adjacent walls. Surely the inescapably trivial act of walking behind a white woman could not justify a Black man's death! I found the marker for Emmett Till, lynched in Money, Mississippi, his body tossed off a bridge over the Tallahatchie River. Mamie Till bravely displayed her son's mutilated body in an open casket at his 1955 funeral in Chicago, exposing this country's racist shame for the whole world to judge. Then, I located a lynching in my childhood Virginia county, Albemarle, from 1898. A total of 150 white men wrestled innocence-protesting John Henry James from a train transporting him to Charlottesville for trial. He assaulted a white woman—allegedly.[3] They shot him and

---

[3] "John Henry James Lynched in Virginia by 150 Unmasked White Men," *Equal Justice Initiative: A History of Racial Justice*, accessed March 10, 2021, https://calendar.eji.org/racial-injustice/jul/12.

hung him by a noose from a tree next to the tracks. For many days, John's "strange fruit" body hung overhead, a warning to Black passersby.

I followed the rust-encrusted steel pendulums along the sloping walkway that ushered hushed visitors into the building's heart: its central green hill. The memorial's *via dolorosa* spiraled, mazelike, downward and inward into a Calvary moment. At the final turn, the covered ramp opened to the sky, blue that morning, benign above a square patch of lush lawn. The docent whispered to me that the hilltop exposure intentionally re-created the terror lynching victims faced. A mob, enraged and unstoppable in its insane and inhuman hate, would have surrounded them. Standing on that rise, I felt exposed and vulnerable even on a peaceful morning.

The parallels to Jesus' passion were unmistakeable: the bloodthirsty crowd had screamed to Pontius Pilate for his death: "Crucify him!" When Pilate ordered the execution to placate their lust, soldiers force-marched Jesus uphill to Golgatha, the skull place of his crucifixion. Goaded by the mob, the soldiers hung him on a tree. He was mocked, whipped, stretched out, and pierced in an excruciating death. As in other moments of this pilgrimage journey, I connected violence against people of color with Christ's crucifixion. The message was clear: Human beings over and over have refused to tolerate God's outstretched arms, which open to embrace people who are poor, strangers, threatening in their difference, or simply exploitable. In the liminal space on a hill under the Alabama sun, Good Friday again became real and urgent: "Were you there when they crucified my Lord?"

Leaving the consecrated memorial grounds, subdued and pensive, I considered how to honor the thousand human lives violently extinguished. Small as it was, I tried not to call the National Peace and Justice Memorial by its colloquial label, the "lynching museum." The people whose lives were brutally stolen deserve more respect. I wanted to lift up their memories as the cost of injustice in America. I hugged their humanity to my heart, confessing the sins of my white culture's quest for domination and possession, possession of everything possible, from riches to land to other people. By the tyranny of white culture, African Americans have been terrorized and brutalized. For the color of their skin, they were killed. "Blood on the leaves and blood at the root."

Before we exited the memorial, our group sang a poignant Litany of the Saints under the blue sky that morning: "All you holy men and women, pray for us." The Catholic ritual, with its chant-like refrain, reinforced the holiness of human life. A cloud of witnesses surrounded us. We said their names and sheltered their wounds within our hearts. Then we directed our steps toward Montgomery, the cradle of the Civil Rights Movement.

The century between the Civil War and the Civil Rights Movement was an abysmal time. Literally, it was a time of darkness. A chaotic time. Chaos can also be a creative, kairos time, if we respond to the winds of the Spirit who stirs the moment with possibility. It had happened in our country: lynchings and Jim Crow segregation birthed the most momentous decades in United States history. Black men and women launched a revolution in the Deep South against the legal and cultural tyranny that had held them in bondage for centuries. In the kairos time of the 1950s and 1960s, African Americans lived as a prophetic community witness for the United States and the world. They caused the "plenty good trouble," which John Lewis spoke about. Upheaval across the American South sparked a new wave of legislation at all levels of government. Deep South revolutionaries sang, marched, and protested to express a Christian vision for a new people and a new nation fully beloved of God. They were joined by people of all races and faiths, and by people of good will, who together felt the righteous power of justice.

March with me into the heart of the Deep South revolution. *Shema!*

Moment 2: Feet and Faith in Montgomery

To orient myself in Alabama's capital city, I walked the short mile along tree-lined sidewalks from the Peace and Justice Memorial past the Freedom Rides Museum in the former Greyhound station to the Dexter Avenue King Memorial Baptist Church. Here and in the Holt Street Baptist Church not far away, Montgomery's Black citizens had prayed and fortified themselves through 382 weary bus-boycott days in 1955 and 1956. The facade of the church, as beautiful now as it was nearly 70 years ago, boasted five arched stained-glass windows, simple and restrained in their patchwork-quilt colors. In the white-walled sanctuary, stark and regimented pews faced the pulpit from which a surprisingly young Rev. Dr. Martin Luther King Jr. had joined other African American pastors and leaders in those roiling protest days.

From the church's white-stepped entry, looking east up Dexter Avenue one block, I saw the classical dome of the Alabama State Capitol, the elegant highpoint of an expansive government complex. Walking along the Capitol's northern flank, I paused before the Confederate Memorial Monument.[4] It commemorated those who had fought and died in the Southern states' treasonous secession from the Union. Ironically, the female figure named Patriotism graced the monument's central 85-foot column. The male figures at the base wore uniforms representing the regiments of the Atillery, Navy, Infantry, and Cavalry that fought for the South. The monument was installed in 1898 as part of the propaganda war when, across this county, Civil War monuments, flags, and leaders' names were plastered in public places to press the ideology of white supremacy. In the same theme, across Washington Avenue from the Capitol stood the First White House of the Confederacy, well preserved. The Confederacy's president, Jefferson Davis, had lived

---

[4] For information about the Confederate Memorial Monument, see *The Encyclopedia of Alabama*, accessed August 28, 2021, http://encyclopediaof alabama.org/article/h-3086.

here until the capital was moved to Richmond in 1861. The historical marker provided dates when the house was occupied but offered no context. It failed to explain that 150 years ago the 13th Amendment specifically outlawed "involuntary servitude" and that Union forces had vanquished the Confederacy along with all it stood for. Civil War memorabilia and Confederate monuments prolonged the dream of white supremacy, effectively denying the Confederacy's loss through a public veneration of its leaders and symbols.

The Capitol building's south-facing plaza boasted a magnificent, spare arc displaying the fifty state flags. The morning I visited, they flapped in a genial breeze, with Alabama's flag as the first in line. Curious. Was this because Alabama deserved premier honors, or did every state just put itself first? Maybe it was simply first in alphabetical order. In my mind the state's citizens deserved pride of place. Sixty years ago, Alabama's brave citizens in Montgomery, in Birmingham, and in Selma led our country in the Civil Rights victories. I heard people say: "Alabama saved America from itself." Amen!

So many other civic lessons vied for my attention in the small circumference of central Montgomery. After a short two-block stroll from the Capitol, I found myself at the Civil Rights Memorial, an imposing engraved roster of brave heroes. Water flowed from the central black granite testament, whose etched script chronicled the movement's sacrificed lives. I located a tribute to Rev. Bruce Kindler, a citizen of Ohio, who was killed in 1970 protesting segregated schools in Cleveland's Glenville neighborhood. Behind the dark stone slab, on the backdrop wall, I read again the prophetic promise of flowing justice, which was Dr. King's talisman in turbulent times: "We will not be satisfied 'until justice rolls down like waters and righteousness like a mighty stream.'" Yes, a fierce and unshakable trust in God's justice sustained the Civil Rights marchers' every step.

A few more downtown blocks brought me to the Legacy Museum, sponsored by the Equal Justice Initiative. Maya

Angelou's words graced the outside wall: "History, despite its wrenching pain, cannot be unlived, but if faced with courage, need not be lived again." Her meaning gripped me: as Americans, regardless of our ancestors' roles, none of us can avoid our past and present sins that flow from racism (slavery, Jim Crow, segregation, mass incarceration, or environmental injustice). Angelou was saying that a more just future begins with an eyes-wide-open grasp of what has happened and where we truly are in terms of racial caste privileges and burdens. This is facing our story with courage: she might have closed her warning words with "*Shema!*"

In the second floor conference room of the museum, I located the tribute that complemented the oxidized coffin markers of the memorial not far away. Row upon row of soil-filled jars lined up on simple wood shelves, with scarcely more explanation than a few white-script words on each. The jars contained holy ground from sites across the country. From the sacred places where men, women, and children were lynched, mourners collected earth into large glass jugs. In a healing ritual, with solemn respect, they cradled the soil-filled jars to their final rest in Montgomery. Anguish and human depravity from America's past were excavated and displayed, transmuted into a powerul summons to justice. The soil colors were a rainbow of honey, rust, sand, charcoal, wheat, cocoa, cinnamon, coffee, copper, and bronze, oddly paralleling the adjectives used to describe the skin tones of people of African descent. In a prayerful pause at the holy shrine, I recollected Cain and Abel in the Genesis story. Cain tried to hide from God calling to him, while his brother's blood at the same moment cried to God for justice from the soil itself. The holy ground collected on the shelves also clamored for justice.

I had one more stopover in Montgomery, a recollection moment with Rosa Parks. The museum bearing her name marked the site of her arrest on December 1, 1955. It expanded the information on a nearby downtown sidewalk marker, which simply identified where she had boarded the city bus. The glass-and-steel three-story building on Troy University's campus chronicled the bus boycott to help visitors imagine the events. A vintage yellow-and-green bus announced its destination from that evening: Cleveland Avenue. One of the nineteen station wagon taxis that had ferried people to work was also preserved. I wondered how many thousands of pairs of dusty, down-at-heel shoes it would take to represent the millions of footsteps along Montgomery streets in 1956. A few yards away in the same exhibit hall, a replica of the Holt Street Church invited me to enter the protest, to feel the promise of hope that sustained the suffering of tired souls and tired soles. I rested my feet in the sanctuary, humbled by the marchers' courage.

> "They came to see that, in the long run, it is more honorable to walk in dignity than to ride in humiliation. . . . [T]he nonviolent approach does something to hearts and souls of those committed to it. It gives them new self-respect. It calls up resources of strength and courage that they did not know they had. Finally, it so stirs the conscience of the opponent that reconciliation becomes a reality."
>
> Martin Luther King Jr., "Pilgrimage to Non-violence"[5]

More than a weary seamstress, Rosa Parks was a trained community activist, prepared in nonviolent resistance and deeply formed within a faith-filled justice-seeking community. When the kairos moment arrived, she was prepared, but she was also fed up with the injustices that held this country captive. Of that night, Parks recounted: "I was just tired of giving in. Somehow, I felt that what I did was right by standing up to that bus driver. I did not think about the consequences. I knew that I could have been lynched, manhandled, or beaten when

---

[5] Martin Luther King Jr., "Pilgrimage to Non-violence," in *Strength to Love* (Minneapolis: Fortress Press, 2010), 160–61.

the police came. I chose not to move. When I made that decision, I knew I had the strength of the ancestors with me."[6] In
her boycott moment, she declared independence anew for
African Americans and for all people who were second-class
human beings in the land of the free. Her defiant refusal to
relinquish her seat for white riders immediately became a
symbol of the Deep South revolution, just like the Boston Tea
Party was for the 1776 revolution, but the story is deeper than
a headline.

The Montgomery Women's Political Council had been peti-
tioning the city for changes to bus segregation policies. Reverend King spoke to a crowd of thousands on the evening of
December 4 in the Holt Street Baptist Church, a few days after
Parks's arrest. While the WPC had initially mobilized African
American residents for a one-day boycott, his rhetoric cemented their resolve to boycott buses until the city permanently eliminated bus segregation. People walked, carpooled,
hailed taxis, and biked to jobs in the city. Despite threats, fines,
injunctions, and violence, even when the boycott leaders were
jailed, the people's courage held firm. Only after the U.S. Supreme Court outlawed segregation on public buses in late 1956
did the Montgomery protesters vote to end the boycott after
thirteen punishing months. This triumph yielded additional
fruit in the passage of the Civil Rights Acts of 1957 and 1960,
the first laws to protect the rights of African Americans since
the Reconstruction and Civil War Amendments.

Rather than being the end of the revolution, the boycott and
subsequent legislation were more akin to a declaration of
independence—emancipation—with bloody fighting to follow.
I needed to pace more deeply into the Deep South revolution
to grasp the moments that changed America.

No buses now—walk with me! *Shema!*

---

[6] Rosa Parks with Gregory Reed, *Quiet Strength: The Faith, the Hope and the
Heart of a Woman Who Changed a Nation* (Grand Rapids: Zondervan, 1994),
23–24, cited in Barbara Holmes, *Joy Unspeakable: Contemplative Practices of the
Black Church* (Minneapolis: Fortress Press, 2017), 132.

Moment 3: "You Do It to Me"

The next moment on this color-line pilgrimage took me to "Bombingham," as Birmingham was tragically nicknamed because so many Black residents' homes had been bombed in the 1960s. My particular destination was the Sixteenth Street Baptist Church. At the historic intersection of 16th Street and 6th Avenue in north-central Birmingham, my slow-moving gaze embraced the church's triple-arched facade, the Kelly Ingram Park, and the Birmingham Civil Rights Institute. The three institutions at this corner overlapped in the narration of noteworthy Civil Rights battles waged in the city decades ago, but for me the grace of Birmingham became distilled in a single tableau.

On September 15, 1963, a Ku Klux Klan bomb exploded at the church just as Sunday morning worship began. Four young girls perished, torn asunder in a jarring white rebuff of their excitement and hopes that morning. A dozen or more people suffered injuries as the lead glass windows shattered, sending colored splinters into the congregation and out to the sidewalk. The damage has been repaired and the windows replaced, but the moment will not ever be forgotten. In the bombing's aftermath, to honor the girls and all who had died struggling for justice, the nation of Wales gifted the church a remarkable stained glass window. The window, installed above the choir loft, proclaimed God's boundless grace through the image of a dark-skinned Jesus. The blunt inscription seared my heart: "You do it to me." I also heard Jesus speaking about his death by lynching: "I do this for you."

Across the Deep South, courageous revolutionaries of all identities had been protesting segregation in the streets and in the courts for nearly a decade. The year 1963 was a momentous one. The country had witnessed the harassment of waylaid, beaten, and killed freedom riders who had traveled on Trailways buses through two-lane Georgia, Alabama, and Mississippi highways. That spring, Dr. Martin Luther King Jr. stirred over 200,000 Civil Rights marchers in Washington, D.C., with his icon words: "I have a dream." In an Alice-through-the-looking-glass parody, Alabama Governor George Wallace chillingly trumpeted "segregation forever" that same year. Medger Evers, NAACP voting rights activist in Mississippi, was assassinated in June by a white man who was not convicted until three decades later. In December, President John F. Kennedy was assassinated, and Lyndon Baines Johnson was installed as his successor.

In Birmingham itself that year, the Southern Christian Leadership Conference (SCLC) had initiated a series of nonviolent direct action campaigns. The campaigns were ultimately successful in challenging discrimination in this, the nation's most segregated, city. King and other SCLC leaders recruited and trained students, even grade schoolers, for nonviolent protests in segregated stores, restaurants, and parks. Disturbing images of fire hoses and police dogs snarling at peaceful protesters in Kelly Ingram Park confronted the nation in newspapers and on nightly television news. Hate—racial hate, white hate—against African Americans was on full display. King was arrested on April 12 and spent days in the Birmingham City Jail, where he penned his famous letter challenging the too-gradual pace of justice counseled by white clergy.

The Sixteenth Street Baptist Church prominently figured in the Children's Crusade as young students in groups of fifty marched from the church to city hall just blocks away.[7] Their objective was to protest segregation by speaking with city leaders about its constraining impact on their lives. People around the world watched in horror at the televised images of Birmingham children being pummeled by fire hoses. Photos of the melees showed dark skin wrinkling under the water's punishing force. Though there was no sound, African American children were plainly screaming in raw terror. The children,

---

[7] See *The Children's Crusade*, accessed August 27, 2021, https://nmaahc.si.edu/blog/childrens-crusade.

arrested by the thousands, filled the jail cells in Birmingham, bringing ever more media attention to segregation and international outrage against this country. The Civil Rights Act prohibiting discrimination in public services was drafted that year and signed into law the following summer by President Johnson.

Saving the sanctuary tour for last that morning, I first sauntered through the Birmingham Civil Rights Institute, not exactly sure what wisdom it would offer to me for my recollection journey. I learned about Birmingham's proud justice history. I experienced vicariously the police intimidation tactics that clogged the jails with old and young protesters. I was drawn particularly to the bomb-mutilated remnants of the windows that had originally adorned the Sixteenth Street Baptist Church nave. The displays preserved a few squares of twisted lead surrounding gaping voids. Ornately scrolled side panels set off the broken center panes of dawn-pink or coffee-tan glass. On one gray metal display table, I saw a quilt-like translucent square. Its central motif, a milky orb, was squared off and reframed in slate-blue and olive-green pieces of glass. Underneath the broken window, a honeyed wood panel interpreted the meaning of the church bombing in gold script: "Then shall he answer them, saying, verily I say unto you inasmuch as ye did it not to one of the least of these, ye did it not to me" (Matt 25:45). In one exhibit after another, many proud faces, resolute and stern, declared to visitors the deadly seriousness of the protest years. People were battling for freedom just as British colonists and their servants had in the 1776 revolution. But instead of resisting taxation without representation, the Deep South revolutionaries fought for basic human dignity, rights of first-class citizenship, and a life free from violence and terror at the hands of their government and fellow citizens.

Leaving the Civil Rights Institute before the school buses arrived, I meandered across Kelly Ingram Park, stopping to read each reenactment and hero story. At one point my pace quickened and I nearly started running. Although I had seen the news clips of police confronting protesters in this park, my stomach nevertheless churned as the cobbled path led me through a disturbingly real dramatization. German shepherds sculpted out of black stone bared their teeth, frozen mid-lunge with open jaws ready to crush young protesters. My own imagination supplied the growls. I experienced an uncomfortable adrenaline surge that was tinged with acrid fear. My breathing only slowed when I reached the far end of the park and stopped to study the butterfly-etched memorials to the Sixteenth Street Baptist Church girls. Addie Mae Collins, Carol Denise McNair, Carole Robertson, and Cynthia Wesley died just as they were poised on the edge of life. They were daughters, sisters, and friends. Had they lived, I thought, they would be cherishing their grandchildren, grandchildren who would be enjoying the freedoms they had purchased with their blood. They carried on their youthful shoulders the community's hope that this time "a change is gonna come," in the words of Sam Cooke's immortal recording.[8]

"[Jesus] also said to the crowds, 'When you see a cloud rising in the west, you immediately say, "It is going to rain"; and so it happens. And when you see the south wind blowing, you say, "There will be scorching heat"; and it happens. You hypocrites! You know how to interpret the appearance of earth and sky, but why do you not know how to interpret the present time?' "

Luke 12:54-56

Next I crossed the intersection to the church. The serene, golden-brick Sixteenth Street Baptist Church presented a striking counterpoint to its significance as a place of deadly racial

---

[8] See Sam Cooke, "A Change Is Gonna Come," provided to YouTube by Universal Music Group, video, 3:13, accessed September 1, 2021, https://www.youtube.com/watch?v=Z5zDRtEC0x0.

violence. Members of this well-heeled congregation, worshipping in the oldest African American church in Birmingham, had prayed, marched, and shed blood to protest discrimination and oppression in their city decades ago. But I felt only tranquility. I gazed up the empty steps to the wide front entrance flanked by imposing square towers. The royal blue neon sign was suspended over the sidewalk and, as it had for decades, blessed the pedestrians who paced beneath it. I heard behind me a steady stream of cars, people going about the business of everyday life, unaware of the grace on display right here.

I entered the church through the basement exhibition area. A generous and gregarious member of the congregation described the simple exhibits that preserved newspaper clippings, ministers' portraits, and community events from the 1960s and beyond. She shared the story of that fateful September morning, pointing out the doorways and passageways that the dynamite had splintered. Then, I reverently climbed the side stairs from the basement to the red-carpeted sanctuary. Majestic organ pipes loomed over the dais, positioned to guard the flag-decorated pulpit and protect those who broke open the Word of God. I imagined Reverend King's mighty voice filling the cavernous hall, thrilling listeners' hearts with prophetic but determined hope. I saw several tourists approaching the pulpit to place themselves in King's shoes, but to me that felt too familiar, lacking a gravitas sufficient to the holy deeds of the courageous community that had worshipped here.

At last, I turned my eyes to the sanctuary's treasure, the leaded-glass window at the back of the church. I knew what image to expect, but my expectations were completely inadequate. From the balcony heights, the blue-white window of a crucified Christ blessed and challenged every person who entered here. I felt embraced by Christ in that moment. Worked in spare detail, his brown-skinned body hung from the cross, back and shoulders rounded, with head fallen forward, sinking to his chest. A halo of light emanated into the world from his heart. "[H]e bowed his head and gave up his spirit" (John 19:30).

In Christ's open arms, I recognized God's cosmos-embracing love, breathed out, washing over the world, and baptizing it ever again, always new. As at the genesis of creation, God's breath was stirring the earth's chaotic darkness once again into hopeful promise. I recognized Love lifted up on the cross, balanced on the horizon between heaven and earth, filling all things with life. I recognized the inscription's truth: "You do it to me." At last, I beheld the truth within the claim I had heard before: Jesus is Black.

"Sometimes we must interfere. When human lives are endangered, when human dignity is in jeopardy, national borders and sensitivities become irrelevant. Whenever men or women are persecuted because of their race, religion, or political views, that place must—at that moment—become the center of the universe."

Elie Wiesel, Nobel Prize Speech, December 10, 1986[9]

Exiting the Sixteenth Street Baptist Church, I recognized a powerful pattern of hope in Birmingham's story. Once the most segregated city in the nation, in 2020 it boasted about its elected African American mayor and how it had developed into a modern city with strength in banking and education, arts and culture. Birmingham had converted its tragedies into power for just change. Lifted up by Birmingham's witness, I turned then to face Bloody Sunday in Selma, the next moment recollecting the Deep South revolution.

[9] Elie Wiesel—Acceptance Speech, NobelPrize.org, Nobel Prize Outreach AB 2021, accessed September 1, 2021, https://www.nobelprize.org/prizes/peace/1986/wiesel/26054-elie-wiesel-acceptance-speech-1986/.

Moment 4: Proud Selma

Selma's gift to the redemption of the nation was the 1967 voting rights march across the Alabama River, followed by sixty-five courageous miles to Montgomery. Selma had glowed in my mind as a beacon of transformation—an inflection point in the Deep South revolution for racial justice. I couldn't wait to walk across the Edmund Pettus Bridge myself. As any pilgrim would, I longed to walk on holy ground and be bathed in the courage of the marchers.

For this recollection moment, I approached Selma not by foot but by car, speeding past scrubby cotton fields on both sides of the road. In the late fall, long straight rows of just-harvested plants ran perpendicular to the two-lane highway. Bushes of stripped stems with withered leaves dotted the coppery-tan ground. Acres of burr-sharp cotton bolls had for centuries been hand-harvested by Black fieldworkers, first as enslaved people and then, later, as freed sharecroppers. Finally, by the 1960s and '70s, huge machine harvesters replaced the sun-scorching, backbreaking, hand-stinging labor. On that morning, tufts of cotton hung on some stems or blew in a desultory way until they were captured by the weedy roadside grasses. I wondered how the cotton felt, so I pulled over to gather some raw fibers, greasy and gritty on my fingers. The fibers had separated from the stinging burrs that scarred the hands and disfigured the fingers of people condemned to work this land for the plantation owners' gain.[10]

For centuries, exhaustive and grueling human labor has been needed to produce cotton, the ancient and luxurious cloth. Cotton begins as a tight white bud with long fibers that must be coaxed from the boll. Cotton was cherished because its

[10] Resmaa Menakem vividly describes his grandmother's hands, scarred and misshapen from picking cotton. *My Grandmother's Hands: Racialized Trauma and the Pathway to Mending Our Hearts and Bodies* (Las Vegas: Central Recovery Press, 2017).

labor-intensive production—from harvesting through ginning, spinning, weaving, and dyeing—made it rare and valuable. However, British spinning and milling inventions in the 1600s sparked the worldwide cotton industry that birthed global capitalism and the European lust for empire building. First in the West Indies, then across the American continents, cotton plantations were seeded by European entrepreneurs and worked by enslaved Africans and their descendants. Growers and manufacturers depended on cheap raw cotton picked and cleaned at greater and greater rates. Even the ingenuity of laborers to plant and pick more cotton was used against them, as overseers lashed the pickers' daily quotas higher and higher. Men, women, and children worked feverishly from sunup to sundown as the cotton market's greed ground them down into the soil.[11]

The drive to Selma led me through infamous Lowndes County. It was known in the 1960s as "Bloody Lowndes" because of the white violence there that suppressed the African American vote. Of its 15,000 residents in 1965, 80 percent were Black people, 80 percent of those individuals lived below the federal poverty line, and not a single African American was registered to vote. In addition to physical intimidation through violence, white landowners and business owners evicted Black tenants from their homes and fired them from their jobs when they tried to vote. This economic pressure was like a long, slow lynching. It was fear-inducing violence applied to individuals and their families as a lever of social domination. Passing the woody hollows separating open fields, I peered up twisting tree-screened driveways, merely tire tracks in rutted red Alabama soil. Even a half century later, the area seemed threateningly remote, hushed, closed to outsiders.

Before crossing the bridge into Selma, I paused first to visit the National Voting Rights Museum and Institute. The weed-

---

[11] Edward E. Baptist, *The Half Has Never Been Told: Slavery and the Making of American Capitalism* (New York: Hachette UK, 2016).

sprinkled white gravel parking lot, desolately quiet that day, edged up to the entrance. The building's humble exterior (it was a converted carpet store) belied the depth and dignity of the museum's mission. Its historic location at the foot of the Edmund Pettus Bridge conferred authority and legitimacy to the stories preserved there. In newsreel clips of Bloody Sunday, I had spied the building's glass-walled exterior in the background as a backdrop for the violent confrontation—police batons against the marchers' heads. Inside now, the three modest exhibit halls of carefully curated photos, documents, and firsthand accounts chronicled the battles in the 1960s to pass the Voting Rights Act. The museum paid tribute to leaders and organizers of the cause, like James Forman and James Bevel, as well as to foot soldiers, like Marie Foster, who showed up for justice on a March Sunday afternoon a lifetime ago.

The protest march on Sunday, March 7, 1965, was deemed "Bloody Sunday" because of the four people who died at the hands of the police that afternoon. The planned march protested the murder of Jimmie Lee Jackson, a voting rights activist shot and then beaten by state troopers in February, just a month before. Along with a dozen others injured, Jackson had been transported to Good Samaritan Hospital in Selma but died after eight days. About six hundred marchers organized for another voting protest march at the Brown Chapel AME Church just a few blocks from the bridge. Clergy from around the nation, from all faiths, joined the march in solidarity to protest the country's refusal to recognize the human dignity and civil rights of African Americans. Armed with batons and tear gas, state troopers stood menacingly at the far end of the bridge. Chaos erupted as the marchers stepped on to the highway. Although the marchers were peaceful, the police beat them, causing dozens of people to be hospitalized. Representative John Lewis, then a twenty-five-year-old activist, was among the most severely beaten; for the rest of his life he coped with the effects of a concussion from that day.

"Walking across the bridge in Selma with my sixteen-year-old daughter in 2011, led by Congressman John Lewis, remains one of the most vibrant and inspiring memories of my life. Mr. Lewis started the Congressional Civil Rights Pilgrimage in 1998 to make sure that his Democratic and Republican colleagues put aside their differences for one weekend every March to travel to Alabama to honor the struggle for civil rights in Birmingham, Montgomery, and Selma. 'Come walk in my shoes,' he always said. John Lewis loved sponsoring young people to join the pilgrimage, and it was because I offered to be a chaperone for a group of high school students that I had the great fortune to go to Alabama. He remains for me a great mentor in learning to lead a life grounded in peace, justice, and love."

> Margaret M. Russell,
> unpublished personal recollection, February 10, 2021

On March 9, again protesters gathered. Rev. Martin Luther King Jr. led twenty-five hundred people to the crest of the Edmund Pettus Bridge. They decided to turn back before reaching the end of the bridge, unwilling to risk senseless beatings once again without federal protection. But that was not the end of the struggle. The protest finally succeeded on March 21 with state and federal protection. Although eight thousand people gathered at the Brown Chapel AME Church to march to Montgomery, only three hundred were allowed to camp overnight on the days-long trek across Lowndes County. The brave Civil Rights foot soldiers walked for five days, singing to bolster their courage against white hecklers on the road shoulder. Twenty-five thousand protesters swelled the march on its final day into Montgomery, where King delivered his famous "How Long, Not Long" speech.

Inspired by the heroic stories and the righteous cause, I eagerly strode across the empty, mud-cratered parking lot toward the bridge incline. The bridge's iconic steel canopy marked the crest of the span. From this height, freedom marchers would have beheld a phalanx of state troopers armed with cold-eyed hate and heavy batons. When I stood at the center of the bridge, I twirled in a circle, deliberately taking in the empty sidewalk beside the lanes of traffic and the slow, muddy flow of the the Alabama River leisurely slipping by underneath me. A tangled, trackless forest of fallen leaves and broken branches formed a formidable boundary on the southern bank of the river, across from the steep cliffs at the city's edge. On the heights of the cliffs, weathered but gracious antebellum facades stood sentinel beside abandoned brick buildings with plywood windows. Rusting fences kept wanderers away from the ridge. Here and there, new construction signaled hope in a revival that still might happen. Nevertheless, a sinking feeling of desolation and abandonment seeped into my heart. I could not reconcile what I saw from the bridge with the Selma of my imagination: proud, defiant, and unstoppable.

I walked pensively through central Selma along Broad Street, planning to stop at the Edmundite Community and then cut over a few blocks to Brown Chapel. The desolate phrase "left behind" circled in my mind.[12] The city's dire poverty was readily visible in the crumbling downtown buildings and the rutted neighborhood streets everywhere. At least a third of the buildings along the key thoroughfares were boarded up and vacant. The Good Samaritan Hospital near the bridge had long since been shuttered and was now an empty hulk with overgrown bushes and dead tree limbs on the lawns. The nearest health clinic was located on the north edge of town. During a brief stop at the Edmundite Community, an order of Roman Catholic priests, a mission officer narrated stories of Selma life in recent decades. She showed off the community's chapel with its

---

[12] Alice Miranda Ollstein, "The Dark Side of Selma the Mainstream Media Ignored," *Think Progress*, March 10, 2015, https://archive.thinkprogress.org /the-dark-side-of-selma-the-mainstream-media-ignored-b7a47d7de749/.

mural honoring the Ugandan martyrs. The community's main mission was feeding Selma residents at the Bosco Nutrition Center. Food insecurity threatened many families because fresh food markets were few and far between in the city center, and many residents could not afford what fresh food there was. Because even police officers and municipal service workers earned minimum wage, they accepted meals at Bosco to make ends meet. The Edmundites had been partnering with municipal offices to build a new recreation center, especially for Selma's youngsters. Unfortunately, as with so much in 2020, the pandemic delayed its opening.

Facts about Selma in 2020

- 43 percent of the population lives in poverty.
- More than 50 percent of the workforce lives in poverty.
- 2/3 of students graduate from high school.
- 70 percent of school children live in single-parent homes.
- The unemployment rate is 14 percent.
- 29 percent of the population suffers food insecurity.[13]

My final destination in Selma was the Brown Chapel AME Church. I walked very slowly along streets lined with gutted storefronts. A cavernous emptiness weighted my heart. It felt like a profound void that could only be filled by a promise of unconditional love and affirmation. Who would say to Selma, as God said to Israel in the Old Testament, "You are my delight"? The George Washington Carver Homes Projects, next to the church, showed little activity that day. Alone or in small clusters, people were coming and going on daily errands. In the 1960s, this community had been bustling, known as the

---

[13] See "Our Challenges," *Edmundite Missions*, 2021, https://www .edmunditemissions.org/our-challenges.

"face of the Civil Rights Movement." Its residents faithfully hosted SCLC leaders in their homes as they descended to Selma to plan voting rights campaigns. Time had erased most signs of the Civil Rights battles that were waged on these streets and the proud marchers who had congregated in its sanctuary. Now, the corner marquee of the chapel announced Sunday's upcoming sermon and worship times. Its tranquil visage, elegantly proportioned, seemed to bless the slow-moving neighborhood. Below the grand facade, I prayed in thanksgiving for the heroic congregation whose moral audacity decades ago had changed the course of this nation. Only the solemn gaze of the silent twin bell towers high above my head witnessed my pilgrimage to pay respect to the freedom fighters now spread to the winds.

The beacon of justice that Selma *should* have become haunted my imagination. As an outsider, visiting briefly without any deep connection to the community, perhaps I had missed something. Older Selma residents whom I joined for lunch at the Bosco Center retold their deeds from the stirring Civil Rights days. They were proud that they had marched into history and that their marching had secured the right to vote for African American citizens. They were proud that their walking-praying feet had bent the moral arc of the universe. Every year, tens of thousands of marcher-tourists still descend on Edmund Pettus Bridge to walk in their footsteps. The crowds revel in reenacted triumph over the bridge span, and then, according to the residents, they leave until the next anniversary and media exposé.

The cost of Selma's proud protest was shockingly high from what I could tell. For fifty-five years, Selma has received little federal or state relief from the grinding poverty of those who call this city home. Many residents, mostly African American, live lives as harsh and segregated in this millennium as they had under Jim Crow. It was not just that our nation had moved on from Selma and the unfinished business of racial rebalancing. Selma seemed to have been abandoned, ignored, and perhaps punished as the nation left the Civil Rights Movement behind. By hosting the protest march all those years ago, the city had become frozen in the public imagination. It symbolized only the bold, freedom-yearning Black voices, intrepid and spirit filled, no longer intimidated by threats of violence. In those days in Selma, Black and white Americans protested to claim full, first-class humanity for the descendants of human beings enslaved on Deep South plantations. No longer would Black Americans stay in their assigned second-class place, they declared with their marching feet. The pride of being Black in America was distilled, clarified, and then mobilized in the sanctuaries of southern churches. Their we-will-move-mountains pride rested on the certain knowledge that they were God's children. They claimed God among them and Jesus as their brother. They trusted deep in their hearts that God had not abandoned them. But the world seemed to have abandoned Selma because of its witness.

On my way back across the Edmund Pettus Bridge, I reflected on how America's original sin displayed itself in heroic Selma. Still, the prophet Isaiah's words reverberated in my heart and tapped out a cadence with my footsteps: "You shall no more be termed Forsaken, / and your land shall no more be termed Desolate; / but you shall be called My Delight Is in Her, / . . . for the Lord delights in you" (Isa 62:4). I wondered: How long until the courageous people of Selma, proud Selma, would be emancipated from unjust, punishing poverty? "Not long!" promised Reverend King a long lifetime ago. I recognized the heroic commitment of the Edmundites and the homegrown leaders, but the city seemed to have been completely left behind, without resources or basic support for its residents. This was the Lower Ninth Ward patttern; this would be the pattern in my hometown too. The righteous struggle for justice has always been an uphill battle, a battle not yet won.

I planned one more *Shema!* moment in Selma, back across the bridge on the other side of the Alabama River. Walk with me!

Moment 5: "What Mean These Stones?"

As I stepped off the Edmund Pettus Bridge sidewalk, with Selma at my back, I turned left into the small memorial park beside Business Highway 80. A series of bronze memorials to Civil Rights leaders greeted me. One particular monument of light gray stones arrested my attention. A dozen angular boulders were set behind a low, wrought iron–fenced perimeter, like those often found at family grave sites. Piled on top of each other, the grouping functioned as a memorial and prayer cairn. These stones appeared sharp, as if recently hewn from a mountainside quarry, natural and arresting. The sizes varied from a towering twelve-foot-tall monolith down to a field rock that a few strong laborers might have shifted by hand. Each stone presented a rugged ashen surface, water-streaked and pitted. I paused to consider the weighty inscription carved in capital letters on the large central stone: "WHEN YOUR CHILDREN SHALL ASK YOU IN TIMES TO COME SAYING, 'WHAT MEAN THESE 12 STONES?' THEN YOU SHALL TELL THEM HOW YOU MADE IT OVER. JOSHUA 4:21-22."

Exactly as the monument designer anticipated, I paused with open eyes and heart. I asked myself: What *did* the stones mean? The verse from the book of Joshua hinted at an audacious endurance that came only from trusting God. Stones suggest strength and bedrock certainty. The grouping here memorialized a community's triumph over adversity, perfectly in line with America's founding story. One generation's sacrifice made possible its descendants' very existence. The verses carved on the stones also hinted at profound reassurance: God's promise, ever again, that God's people would make it over. "We shall overcome." But then I considered the reckoning in our country right now. In the intervening years from 1965 to 2020, America's racial caste system has changed only its weapons, not its aim. The anguished cries of centuries have resounded in cities across the nation this past year: "Stop killing us!" Apparently, "making it over" is an already-but-not-yet promise.

I researched Joshua to understand the twelve-stone story that wrapped up the Exodus epic. The Jordan crossing was not a happily-ever-after ending to the miraculous escape from the pharaoh's overseers. The Israelites' passover out of slavery began with the night flight from Egypt and their pursuers' death upon the shore. That was not the end. The book of Joshua takes up the thread of the story after Moses's death, just as the Israelites emerged from the Sinai wilderness. God selected Joshua to lead the Israelites for the final "passover" into Canaan. All twelve tribes, some forty thousand strong, had to cross the Jordan River's spring torrent safely west into Canaan in that prophetic moment.

Among the tents and animals, among all the baggage that the Israelites had carried through the wilderness, was the ark of the covenant. This holy chest protected the tablets engraved with the law that God had given to Moses. The ark was the enduring sign of God's presence among the people as they traveled day and night. The story of the Jordan crossing reprised the people's Red Sea crossing out of Egypt. In both events, the Lord God miraculously held back swiftly flowing waters so the people could cross safely. To enable the Israelites to ford the Jordan, the Levite priests carried the ark into the river, as the Lord instructed them, and remained in the center of the waters. The presence of the ark stopped the river's flow to create a safe, dry path to pass over. After the people had crossed into Canaan, one man from each of the twelve tribes excavated a large stone from the riverbed. Installed on the Gilgal plain, the twelve stones memorialized for future generations that the tribes had "made it over" the Jordan. But more than recalling a simple fact, the stones reminded the people of *how* they had "made it over"—in God's care.

The verses from Joshua stirred up powerful memories for me. I recalled a momentary exchange from the first year my husband and I were married. It has not lost its poignancy or power even after decades of life together. Not long after our short honeymoon, we moved into our first apartment to finish

professional school. We found a U.S. census form in our apartment mailbox, or maybe we were doing taxes. In any case, the
question asked us to identify the race of our household. We
marked Larry as the head of household, which meant that our
household was "Black." I looked up at him and, thinking I was
witty, remarked: "I used to be white; now I'm Black." Instead
of laughing at the incongruity of his Scotch-Irish wife being
labeled African American, he said gently: "It's OK. You can
leave." Implicit in these few words were two powerful truths.
First, his black skin meant that he could not leave racism behind, but I could choose to. Second, his love for me meant that
he would not leave me behind, no matter how the world would
treat us. Four decades and a lifetime of adventures later, I have
not left, and neither has he. That is how we have made it over.

We don't claim a heroic faithfulness in our lives but rather
a day-in-and-day-out just-making-it commitment. Our marriage has been tested by life's difficulties and human foibles,
just as all marriages are. But America's racism has brought our
family to the breaking point sometimes and broken our hearts
more times than we can count. I have always wanted to shield
my husband and our children from the world that insulted
them, refused their gifts, and undermined their worth. It
wasn't always possible, because to be Black or brown in
American means that you cannot escape indignities and exploitation. However, I also failed because I'm still on the way
to comprehending how this country's racism, including my
own white privilege, is relentless and ever present. Together
Larry and I have protected our children as best we could.
We've tried to arm them with humor, self-esteem, and resilience. To paraphrase the Selma stones, we are making it over.
We get over year by year. We get over because we vowed to
live for one another as partners in the world, and that commitment in solidarity makes all the difference.

In that grace-filled moment in Selma's roadside park, my heart
overflowed with the significance of my husband's I-won't-
leave-you promise. I heard the same promise in snippets and

scraps of Scripture echoing in my memory. God declares to human beings throughout Scriptures, from Exodus to Revelation: "I will take you for my people and I will be your God." I heard it in the Shema: "Hear, O Israel, the Lord our God, the Lord is one." The great prophet Jeremiah promised in the Lord's name: "Look the days are coming. . . . [O]n that day, I will deliver you." Emmanuel means "God with us." Jesus' own name means "God saves." In the face of threats, the Civil Rights marchers sang "Leaning on the Lord!" and "This Little Light of Mine." So what do these snippets of verse and song mean? To me they mean that good and evil vie in creation for power over the human heart. Nevertheless, every fiber of my being also tells me that goodness and love are already defeating hate. We are making it over injustice, already but not yet.

Reverend King shared the same conviction in his potent sermons following the bus boycott in Montgomery and during his periods of imprisonment in Birmingham: "At the center of the Christian faith is the conviction that in the universe there is a God of power who is able to do exceedingly abundant things in nature and in history. . . . The God whom we worship is not a weak and incompetent God. He is able to beat back gigantic waves of opposition and to bring low prodigious mountains of evil." [14] When the burdens of Civil Rights battles pushed King to the end of his stength, he found God there: "At that moment I experienced the presence of the Divine as I had never before experienced him. . . . I could hear the quiet assurance of an inner voice, saying, 'Stand up for righteousness, stand up for truth. God will be at your side forever.'" God did not promise King either safety or success. God's "ableness" did not obviate King's obligation to battle evil with good, to confront violence with peace, and to counter hate with love. Rather, God's faithfulness meant that God is with us. Our God's justice is an already-but-not-yet justice, a co-created

---

[14] Quotations in this paragraph are from Martin Luther King Jr., "Our God Is Able," in *Strength to Love*, 109–17.

justice. Justice in relationship to God and neighbor: that is the summons and the promise.

As I left the Joshua stones, I gathered a shard of gravel from the wrought iron enclosure and balanced it upon a stone within my reach. "What mean these stones?" They meant that God's grace would accompany me as I walked America's color line. I had come this far by faith, and faith would accompany me. With this assurance, with my tokens of hope, I had two more moments of recollection in the Deep South. Once again, walk with me, and let's pay attention! *Shema!*

Moment 6: Mighty Morehouse

After Selma, I traveled to Atlanta to soak up more grace from Reverend King's legacy. His presence was palpable and hard to miss in Atlanta, in the National Center for Civil and Human Rights, the Ebenezer Baptist Church, his childhood home, and the King Center for Nonviolent Social Change. Instead of touring the predictable sites, I chose a road less taken, so to speak; I chose to recollect the Deep South revolution with a moment at Morehouse College, King's alma mater. Morehouse College's unapologetic African American identity has healed Black men's wounds, made them whole, and prepared them for the justice struggles of their time. Morehouse extended that grace to me, a stranger welcomed into its precious, powerful community.

On an overcast, drizzly morning in Atlanta, I first attended a small community Mass at Lyke House, the Catholic student ministry office. Its name honored Archbishop of Atlanta James P. Lyke, the first African American archbishop. Students from Morehouse College, Spelman College, Clark Atlanta University, and Georgia State University, regardless of their racial identity, could find a home within its calm, bright spaces. However, unmistakably, the center's vocation was to celebrate and support young Black Catholics. Lyke House's cruciform architecture, the building's well-selected art, and its entranceway styled like an Ethiopian cross all reinforced the community's African roots. Tiers of small arched windows punctuated the upper reaches of the elegant sanctuary, recalling slender slots cut into the thick stone walls of a desert stronghold.

I could sense immediately how the style of Lyke House linked contemporary African American Catholics with early Christian evangelization stories like the episode in Acts of the Apostles. A brief but well-known vignette in that text describes how the apostle Philip chanced upon the royal manager of the Ethiopian court of Queen Candace (Acts 8:26-40). The eunuch treasurer was studying Hebrew Scriptures to parse their meaning for his own salvation. Philip showed him how Jesus was God's Messiah and then he baptized the new believer by the side of the road. This story—and Lyke House—rebuked me for thinking Blackness was a graft upon white Western Christianity. Rather, long before Christianity became a European religion, African communities along the continent's coasts received the Christian kerygma. Christianity's most ancient roots grew fruitfully in fertile African soil at the very founding of the faith.

As I entered the chapel, a striking gold-on-black icon greeted me. The dark-skinned image was Jesus bedecked as a Maasai warrior surrounded by the Greek Christogram IC XC, signifying Jesus the Christ. The four Evangelists' enfleshed identities (angel, lion, ox, and eagle) adorned the corners of the central medallion. The legend at the bottom venerated Christ as the "Lion of Judah," in the words of Revelation 5:5. The icon preached to me that Jesus is Emmanuel ("God with us") in the guise of a cloak-draped, nomadic herdsman, staff in hand, settled on his heels close to the earth, peering into my heart. The dazzling, dark Christ was the third signpost witness for me from this week in the Deep South. It complemented the blazing, stained glass crucified Christ in the Sixteenth Street Baptist Church and the twelve stones of Selma at a roadside park. We will get over because God is near; God is with us; God dwells within the beating heart of our human communities.

After Mass, on the short walk to Morehouse, I passed students brimming with excitement about the homecoming festivities that afternoon. The chilly mist could not quench their school spirit and rowdy calls. I arrived at campus just in time for an admissions presentation and then a short tour. Morehouse is the only all-men's institution among the fifty-six private historically Black colleges and universities. For over 150 years, the college has educated African American men, preparing them for roles of leadership in church and society. Founded as a seminary in 1867 after the Civil War, students and teachers gathered at first in a church basement. Study in the early years was limited to basic literacy for the men who had been enslaved or else denied formal education because of their African ancestry. Its curriculum and degrees eventually conformed to typical seminary and liberal arts studies at the country's oldest institutions, such as Yale, Harvard, and William and Mary. The college's administration building, classrooms, and dormitories all faced a central quadrangle to provide the students and faculty with the sense of a cohesive learning community. Although Morehouse admits men of any racial or ethnic background, the curriculum foregrounds the perspectives of Americans of color, Africans and their descendants, and Black people across all times and places. A central purpose of the curriculum is to guide students to explore themes relating to justice, liberal arts, society, and power structures.

Although I was not the intended target of the admissions pitch, I recognized how young Black men might luxuriate in an atmosphere that affirmed rather than questioned their worth. They did not have to fear color judgments or feel weighted by a double consciousness under an exacting white gaze. The high school visitors' chatter and laughter bubbled up infectiously as Morehouse student presenters extolled the education and campus life. A Morehouse education layered character formation and leadership experience on top of traditional learning methods to acculturate the graduates to high standards of personal integrity and leadership on a big stage.

Everywhere, signs and buildings chronicled the impressive achievements of Morehouse alumni, similar to liberal arts colleges across the nation. I learned that its graduates are second to none in the annals of American freedom fighters and cultural innovators.

Perhaps I romanticized Morehouse from a single morning's presentation and tour, but the camaraderie and community tugged at me. Even as I sat at the edge of the room, I experienced for a brief moment the warmth of being welcomed and included. As I absorbed the message to visiting high school students, I found a touchstone for understanding. Much of my education and early career as a lawyer had been spent in predominantly male environments. I had been admitted to Yale in one of the first women's classes. The university was not prepared for women, either in its curriculum or its facilities. My law school class at the University of Virginia was predominantly men, as was my "class" of starting associate lawyers at a Cleveland firm. If we wanted to be counted as serious lawyers, we did not speak of marriage or motherhood. When I studied for my PhD in systematic theology at Boston College, I had many women classmates, but women's perspectives were rarely discussed in classes, and when they were, it was mostly as a by-the-way postscript. These were typical experiences for women of my generation as traditionally all-male professions opened to us. We were expected to act and think "like a man," so there was no place for resistance or complaint. Then I linked Morehouse's emancipation for young men of color to the glorious liberation I felt in my first academic job at Ursuline College, a Catholic "women focused" college near Cleveland.

At Ursuline, I joined a faculty mostly of women who were largely of European and Catholic backgrounds. The student body was more diverse in age and ethnicity but still predominantly women. I realized why it felt so comfortable at Ursuline. The college was deliberately fashioned by, for, and through the experiences of women. The graduate and undergraduate curricula were intentionally designed to cultivate women's awareness of identity and voice, as these reinforced reasoning and critical thinking.[15] Professors never needed to justify reading women's writings or to explain why they covered women's issues as their scholarship agenda. Ursuline College unapologetically credited women's experiences (and those of similarly excluded groups). When I moved into administration, new policies were always reviewed in light of their impact on women as caregivers, mothers, nontraditional students, and breadwinners. Being in a community that focused on women taught me about the power of culture to reinforce who counts and who does not. I began to recognize injustice in the air and on the ground in the hidden structures of society and power. My years at Ursuline started to repair my education and heal my spirit. I experienced my gender as a strength and began to recognize that the defects I felt were not mine but were imperfections charged against me by institutions that were designed to conform me to male norms.

Connecting Ursuline and Morehouse, I recognized the power of social critique and of a more inclusive pedagogy. A Morehouse education allowed students to see whiteness as a social category, not a norm, and to learn again the country's history with all people included. They learned how to recognize implicit values and how to recenter full-dimensional humanity as a yardstick of meaning. Against the onslaughts of a dominant white culture sure of its own preeminence, I sensed that Black men at Morehouse, like myself at Ursuline, would find a community that would consider them on their own terms. They would see faces like their own and hear stories that belonged to their ancestors also. They would find safety to cry or rage with other people who had suffered for the color of their skin or the presentation of their bodies. Against the threats of physical violence from police and white

---

[15] The core curriculum was structured on Mary Field Belenky and others, *Women's Ways of Knowing: The Development of Self, Voice, and Mind* (New York: Basic Books, 1986).

vigilantes, they might even find sanctuary here. The simple introduction to Morehouse in an admissions presentation on that fall day allowed me to imagine how this institution might nurture young men of color into bold self-determination. In that rain-gray moment, it seemed that a Black person's breath might flow more freely when they experienced how their lives mattered.[16]

It was time for me to complete my tour of the Deep South revolution. I wanted to find the connections between that time and the reckoning of our nation since 2020. Walk with me to the nation's turning point in the Civil Rights Movement. *Shema!*

Moment 7: 1968

In the final moment of this third week on pilgrimage, I recollected 1968, when events so radically shifted in the Civil Rights Movement. Americans born after 1950 often name that year as the most tumultuous in their memories. The only year that vies for recognition as most socially cataclysmic might be the one we have just endured—2020. Because Martin Luther King was assassinated on April 4, 1968, political historians have taken the year as a pivotal moment in the country's history. I lived through 1968, being just out of elementary school, so I had some hazy memories of that year. I wanted to understand the watershed year as an inflexion point for our nation on its racial justice color-line journey. I took up my shillelagh again, my crucifix, and another talisman expression from Psalm 51: "Deliver me from the guilt of bloodshed, O God, / O God of my salvation, / and my tongue will sing aloud of your deliverance" (v. 14).

---

[16] Just as I edited this recollection moment, I received the news that in May 2021 white competitors had mocked Morehouse's accomplished debate team at an intercollegiate championship. The Morehouse men withdrew in protest. The contest organizers apologized and cancelled the event. Still, the lash stung.

In 1968, America witnessed particularly profound upheavals that shook the nation. Foremost among these was Reverend King's assassination in the early spring. After his nationally televised funeral on April 9, citizens in one hundred cities across the nation protested America's too-slow progress toward justice. In June, just two months later, United States Attorney General Robert Kennedy was also assassinated. Vietnam War protestors marched against the Democratic National Convention in Chicago. Black American athletes held up gloved fists on the Olympic award stand in Mexico City. The country elected Republican Richard Nixon as president, and Apollo 8 orbited the moon on Christmas Eve. It was a tumultuous year.

In the 1960s, race revolution battles were being waged in northern and midwestern cities as well as in the Deep South, because segregation and exploitation were powerful north of the Mason-Dixon Line too. The dated code words still surfaced in my recollection. The media used expressions like "race riots" or "unrest in the urban core" to describe African American citizens' vocal protests against the comprehensive oppression they were suffering. In this decade in particular, non-white citizens suffered rising unemployment, increasingly unequal or declining wages, a widening loss of property values and wealth, and of course, vehemently segregated schools and neighborhoods. There were over 700 race conflicts documented in the years from 1964 to 1967. The people injured totaled 12,000, and 228 people were killed—mostly African Americans. Cities across the country suffered 15,000 incidents of arson, and property damage ran into the hundreds of millions of dollars or more.[17] The National Advisory Commission on Civil Disorders, the Kerner Commission, concluded in 1968 that

---

[17] Kenneth T. Walsh, "50 Years after Race Riots, Issues Remain Largely the Same," *U.S. News and World Report*, July 12, 2017, https://www.usnews.com/news/national-news/articles/2017-07-12/50-years-later-causes-of-1967-summer-riots-remain-largely-the-same.

"white racism" lay at the heart of the violent urban confron-tations.[18]

> "At approximately 1:00 a.m. on March 24, 1970, a bomb irrep-arably damaged the Cleveland museum's [bronze casting] of *The Thinker.* The bomb itself had been placed on a pedestal . . . and had the power of about three sticks of dynamite.
> "No one was injured in the subsequent blast, but the statue's base and lower legs were destroyed. The remaining sections of the cast were blown backward to form a 'plume' at the base, and the entire statue was knocked to the ground. . . .
> "No one was ever arrested or charged with the destruc-tion. . . . [The Museum of Art board] decided that the statue should not be repaired, but placed outside the museum in its damaged condition."
>
> "Rodin's *The Thinker*," The Cleveland Museum of Art[19]

Like so many other average people in those years, my family and my husband's family were foot soldiers in the Civil Rights Movement by virtue of the small but significant choices they made, especially in school and neighborhood desegregation skirmishes. For different family reasons, we were both part of

[18] Walsh, "50 Years." This article states: "The National Advisory Commis-sion on Civil Disorders, known as the Kerner Commission after its chairman, Illinois Gov. Otto Kerner Jr., was appointed by LBJ in July 1967 to study the causes of the riots. In February 1968, the panel concluded, 'Our nation is moving toward two societies, one black, one white—separate and unequal.' The commission found that in the 1967 riots, 83 people were killed and 1,800 injured, most of them African-American, and property valued at more than $100 million was damaged, looted or destroyed. The report blamed 'white racism' as the underlying cause of the violence. And the commission said the riots were largely triggered by confrontations between local police and African-American men."
[19] "Rodin's *The Thinker*," The Cleveland Museum of Art, accessed March 30, 2021, https://clevelandart.org/research/conservation/rodins-thinker.

the racial experiments of the time. At the end of the 1960s, my father's scholarship and teaching agenda revolved around constitutional rights and, more specifically, school integration. When he taught at Northwestern Law School, he moved his family to a liberal suburb of Chicago where schools and neighborhoods were mixing. I attended Haven Junior High School in Evanston[20] for sixth and seventh grades. I walked about eight blocks to school. African American students mostly took the bus. I recall now that my world was solely white—white girls and boys.

Like any adolescent in junior high, I was acutely aware of the pecking order in the halls and at after-school clubs. One event sticks in my mind. Some white students relentlessly teased a classmate, the daughter of German immigrants, who had such dim vision that she held a book inches from her nose to read. African American girls derided the perpetrators by asking why white kids failed to honor and protect their own group. I don't recall joining the mockery, but I also did not stand by our classmate. I felt shamed when we were called out for blatant cruelty. It seemed that we learned early who counted and how to subjugate those who did not. How do I now judge my eleven-year-old self? Well, we stayed in our comfort zone among our own. We practiced segregation and domination at Haven Junior High, not quite realizing how we were recreating our cultural values. We upheld segregation's conventions without really recognizing that this was a choice in itself. Integrating schools meant opening the doors, but we had not learned real inclusion. Teach your children well!

In contrast, in the late 1960s my husband's family moved from Springfield, Massachusetts, to Newton Highlands, a

---

[20] Evanston has been in the news recently for its reparation plans. See Rachel Treisman, "In Likely First, Chicago Suburb of Evanston Approves Reparations for Black Residents," *NPR News*, March 23, 2021, https://www.npr.org/2021/03/23/980277688/in-likely-first-chicago-suburb-of-evanston-approves-reparations-for-black-reside.

close-in, almost all-white suburb of Boston. After years of night school, his father completed his degree in electrical engineering and began a career at a nearby computer company. The family chose Newton to secure opportunities for their children, such as an excellent education and a safe suburban neighborhood. They purchased a modest house that backed up to the trolley line. Families on this street stayed put and became neighbors to the "young Black family" who lived at the center of the block. I met the neighbors years later, when they celebrated our marriage and helped us welcome our children into the world. In the tumultous years of the late 1960s, the street was a haven of good sense and decency. A small step forward on America's color-line journey.

What did 1968 mean as a moment along my color-line pilgrimage? Many things changed and refocused that year. I wish I could say that it was a gigantic step toward racial equity that we enjoy now decades later. Unfortunately, it was a pivot in the worst sense of the word. The nation turned its back on the racial justice struggles of Black Americans and all people of color. The curtain fell on progress for racial equality when King was killed. The United States turned its attention to other wars: the Vietnam War, the war on poverty, and the war on drugs. In each war, the nation blamed the victims, who were mostly poor and marginalized by their color. The American resistance to full racial integration and equality migrated out of the South, following the path of African Americans who fled Jim Crow. In the same way, 1968 directed my steps along the route of the color line—north.

Turning North

The third week of this pilgrimage led me across the Deep South to visit moments of a second American revolution. The week covered huge swaths of ground and time. Leaving sugar plantations of nineteenth-century Louisiana behind, I marched through the terror and grief of lynching into the Deep South's "plenty good trouble," when chaos and courageous sacrifice stirred hopes of just change. As I wrote these gleanings of wisdom from the Deep South week, Christian churches across the globe celebrated the Holy Easter Triduum. Christ's passion-and-death moments were perfectly suited to recollecting the love-emanating "you do it to me" Christ window from Birmingham. Christ's resurrection promised redemption in a kairos–new creation moment, a passover from death to life. Redemption in the risen Christ is already but not yet. Likewise, the Deep South revolution remained unfinished national business.

I decided to pace through my hometown on this color-line pilgrimage and see that city with wide-open eyes. I knew that residents in the suburbs east of Cleveland had tried to respond faithfully to the summons of the Civil Rights Movement. Their already-but-not-yet victories were rarely told. I turned north from the Deep South revolution to see its impact in northern moments of promise and possibility.

Walk with me! Let's move our feet! *Shema!*

Fourth Week
Just Resistance

The fourth week of the color-line pilgrimage brought me home. The moments of this week closed the loop for me on the history and geography of America's original sin. I felt the sweep and weight of my journey. I was ready to gather the Spirit's gifts and gleanings. I was ready to wind down and return to daily life. But I wanted to know more about how communities resisted the divisions of race that America's white culture foisted upon them.

During the first week on pilgrimage, I got my bearings and explored how anti-Black racism and white domination emerged as America's original sin. I also excavated my own founding, so to speak, and the ties that bound my family and myself to America's story. The second week of the color-line pilgrimage connected me with slavery's reign in the nineteenth century and its legacy still visible in New Orleans. On the third week, I visited moments of the Deep South revolution—particularly the Civil Rights Movement—to encounter essential battles in the struggle for racial justice, still unfinished. Likewise, my pilgrimage was not yet complete.

The moments of just resistance this week transported me north, like the Great Migration of millions of Black Americans who journeyed to urban centers, where they hoped to find a freer life. In this week, I visited only sites and shrines in Cleveland, but I might have been almost anywhere in the United States. I chose Cleveland because I knew it well, I thought. Its journey along the color line since the twentieth century has

118

mirrored that of other northern cities, but it detoured from the well-trod path in significant moments. Jim Crow had gripped Cleveland and its suburbs with the same vehemence and viciousness that had gripped southern states, segregating African Americans, exploiting them, and controlling their every move. Then, along a short byway, I stumbled fortuitously into a path of possibility on Cleveland's east side. I saw how a community had chosen to resist segregation. This story needed to be told too. At the end of my race and grace pilgrimage, I paused a final moment to consider how to begin the difficult work of repentance and how to commit my heart to the work of justice.

> "We Americans are among the most sin-sick people on God's earth. Our sickness goes to the very core of this country's being. We will never heal in our government, in our economy and even in our churches until we face the fact that we are sinners who need to accept our history, in its achievements and its failures. We must repent of the sin of racism. Only then may all Americans be healed of our sickness and freed of our demons. Let us be assured that there is a balm in Gilead to heal our sin-sick soul."
>
> Greg Chisholm, SJ, Homily, St. Patrick's Cathedral, NYC[1]

With my walking stick, my crucifix, and the lessons gleaned from my past saunterings, this week I turned north and prepared to finish the color-line odyssey. Walk with me through my hometown of Cleveland Heights, Ohio, to see the witness of justice there decades ago. I learned might be possible in the struggle for racial justice. Walk with me!

---

[1] Gregory Chisholm, SJ, "The Cry of an Angry Black Man in a World Sick with Racism," *America Magazine*, February 12, 2021, https://www.america magazine.org/politics-society/2021/02/12/racism-angry-black-man-homily -240005.

Moment 1: The Cleveland-Glenville Shoot-Out

I left the Deep South in the pivotal year of 1968, with eyes newly opened, to visit Cleveland's Glenville neighborhood "shoot-out," which happened that same year.[2] The Glenville battle between Black Nationalist protesters and law enforcement officers represented one of the many incendiary confrontations that exploded across northern and western American cities during the hot restive summer after Reverend King's assassination. "Urban warfare" erupted in hundreds of the destination cities that received African American migrants from the Deep South. The conflagrations erupted because, when Black refugees arrived, they experienced in northern cities the same kinds of segregation and exploitation that they had expected to leave behind. While its specifics varied, the Black-white color line was as vigorously defended outside the South as it was below the Mason-Dixon Line. Before I visited the shoot-out site, I lingered first over a few episodes where the color line in housing became personal. Then I visited Glenville to see what remained of the shoot-out. I wish I could say that a small, soft voice of hope supported me in that moment, but mostly I felt a bitter blast of disillusionment shaking me, waking me.

The northern battle lines of white backlash against voting rights and racial equality cut through neighborhoods and schools. A person might have thought that northern cities were more progressive about desegregation, but that was not the case when my husband and I tried to find neighborhoods to live in. In the early 1980s we moved into a gracious east-side Louisville neighborhood. New to the city, we walked back to our apartment on a summer morning after Sunday Mass. From out of nowhere, a young white man threatened to kill us as he

---

[2] Lorraine Boissoneault, "What Happened When Violence Broke Out on Cleveland's East Side 50 Years Ago?," *Smithsonian Magazine*, July 24, 2018, https://www.smithsonianmag.com/history/complicated-history-1968-glenville-shootout-180969734/.

walked by, enraged to see white and Black together. Perhaps we were too easily intimidated, but that was enough. From then on, we only ventured out socially in Louisville with allies to accompany us. We made our own great migration further north as soon as our jobs permitted. We lived further from the Deep South, but the same hostility confronted us. In a Philly suburb the next year, we bought a small home with flowering shrubs, leafy trees, and an attached garage. Later we learned that neighbors had gathered signatures for a petition to prevent us from purchasing there. Again, allies protected us, but we heard the message: "We do not want you." In Vermont fifteen years later, vandals on our rural cul-de-sac sent the same shocking message on a chilly night before Halloween. We woke to nasty graffiti and eggs on the house. Firecrackers had exploded our mailbox at the end of the drive. Other families on the street had welcomed us to their homes, so we knew we had allies. Nevertheless, the threat of harm haunted us. These episodes forced us to reexamine the American racial progress story we had been telling ourselves. We began to see that we had lived too credulously into a narrative that the Civil Rights Movement had conquered racism and that only "a few bad apples" remained. America's original sin still shaded this country, and the promised land was still a long way off regardless of where a Black person chose to live. Our story simply exemplified what Black families have experienced over and over again in northern cities. Progress toward racial inclusion is both already, but not yet.

The Great Migration: Many histories of the United States have given short shrift to the Great Migration even though it was among the largest intranational displacement of refugees in world history.[3] The influx of African Americans to the North and West prompted white-dominated legislatures to restrict

---

[3] Isabel Wilkerson, *The Warmth of Other Suns: The Epic Story of America's Great Migration* (New York: Random House, 2010). Wilkerson, the first African American woman to be awarded the prestigious Pulitzer Prize, conducted

the economic, social, and political lives of African Americans in far-reaching ways that still hobble them today. Southern Black refugees anticipated that, in the North, they would live beyond the power and legacy of the Southern slaveholding society. However, white-controlled legislatures enacted laws and policies to control African Americans and limit every sphere of life: housing and mortgages, unemployment and Social Security benefits, Medicare and Medicaid, education, and public facilities.[4] The first, most significant restraint was to segregate neighborhoods and to imprison Black residents in the worst districts of the cities. "Never before had a nation thrived—grown in population and in wealth—while its major cities decayed. [Municipalities and businesses enacted policies] to keep Black residents poor and confined, powerless to improve their neighborhoods and subject to the brunt of urban violence, while whites fled to more prosperous communities."[5] Northern white Americans were as fearful of miscegenation and African American equality as their southern counterparts.

In the decades from the Reconstruction to 1970, between seven and eight million African Americans streamed out of the Deep South along three key routes flowing north or west. From the Carolinas and eastern Georgia, freedmen and women with their families, in the earliest wave after the Reconstruction, headed up the coast to Boston, New York, Philadelphia, and Washington, D.C., as well as to the Tidewater area of Virginia. From Atlanta along the Gulf Coast to the Mississippi River and northward to Arkansas, a second stream of Jim Crow refugees journeyed upriver through the center of the country

---

one thousand interviews over fifteen years to document this moment in America's color-line travels.

[4] Richard Rothstein, *The Color of Law: A Forgotten History of How Our Government Segregated America* (New York: Liveright Publishing, 2017); Daria Roithmayr, *Reproducing Racism: How Everyday Choices Lock in White Advantage* (New York: New York University Press, 2014).

[5] David Stradling and Richard Stradling, *Where the River Burned: Carl Stokes and the Struggle to Save Cleveland* (New York: Cornell University Press, 2015), quoted in Boissoneault, "Cleveland's East Side."

toward Midwestern cities after World War I. They resettled in the urban neighborhoods of Chicago, Gary, St. Louis, Indianapolis, Detroit, Cleveland, and Pittsburgh. In a later wave starting in 1940, African Americans from Texas fanned out to the West Coast, setting their hopes on Seattle, Portland, San Francisco, and Los Angeles. They came to ports and factories that needed laborers to support the country's World War II defense manufacturing industries. They left their southern homelands and families for a myriad of individual reasons, but they had reached their breaking points. Mostly they left to escape Jim Crow segregation, threats of violence both severe and petty, and permanent second-class citizenship in all the forms that shackled their lives. I recalled the National Peace and Justice Memorial in Montgomery. The memorial's hanging coffins spoke with terrifying eloquence of why African Americans "voted with their feet" against the conditions threatening them in the South.

Cleveland-Glenville: Of the millions of southern African American refugees of the Great Migration, over half a million people moved to Cleveland during the twentieth century. The city's population experienced two major surges, one after each World War. During the nineteenth century before the Civil War, most Black residents in Cleveland lived in the integrated Central neighborhood, although there was no real racial equality.[6] Schools, restaurants, civic halls, and businesses generally served a racially mixed clientele. If anything, Cleveland's neighborhoods were enclaves defined by their Catholic ethnic parishes, with immigrants from Poland, Italy, Germany, and Hungary. With the influx of southern Black refugees to Cleveland, especially in the mid-twentieth century, the city enacted strict segregationist policies and later built public housing

---

[6] Enslavement of Africans and their descendants was common across the northern British colonies and in the Western Reserve (now Ohio and nearby states), as was segregation and social exploitation. See, e.g., Rebecca Hall, *Wake: The Hidden History of Women-Led Slave Revolts* (New York: Simon & Schuster, 2021).

units to concentrate and confine its Black residents.[7] The Glen-ville neighborhood had long been the home to Cleveland's Jewish citizens, from the turn of the twentieth century to about 1950, until that group migrated eastward to the suburban towns that allowed non-Christians.[8] Cleveland's African American residents then moved eastward out of Central to Glenville. With the flight of Jewish families out of Cleveland, the percentage of Black residents in Glenville grew from eight percent in 1930 to 90 percent by the 1950s. African American communities on the east side of Cleveland "struggled with schools that weren't fully integrated, dwindling economic opportunities, and regular harassment from the police."[9] Cleveland's problems mirrored those of other urban centers in the country. Its African American neighborhoods were over-crowded with disturbingly poor access to public services like education, law enforcement, and health care.

The Cleveland-Glenville shoot-out took place just a few miles from where I now live. By 1968, Glenville had long been poor, crowded, and restless, as it remained in 2020.[10] In recent years, on summer evenings, my husband and I have often paused to listen to a sharp crack in the distance. We wonder: "Was that a gunshot or fireworks?" We were pretty confident on Fourth of July weekends that we heard fireworks. Other

[7] "The Great Migration," *Cleveland Restoration Society*, accessed May 27, 2021, https://www.clevelandrestoration.org/projects/the-african-american -experience-in-cleveland/the-great-migration.

[8] "Memories of an Old Jewish Neighborhood," *Cleveland Jewish History*, accessed May 27, 2021, https://www.clevelandjewishhistory.net/places /glenville/index.htm.

[9] Boissaneault, "Cleveland's East Side."

[10] The neighborhood was restless that summer for all the reasons that so-ciologists have long detailed. Poverty and violence reinforce each other where people are desperate in overcrowded neighborhoods, abandoned by society with few chances to escape the conditions imposed upon them. Campbell Robertson, "Gunfire and Crashing Cars: In Struggling Neighborhoods, 'We're Losing Our Grip,'" *New York Times*, January 2, 2021, https://www.nytimes .com/2021/01/02/us/crime-poverty-pandemic-cleveland.html.

times, we thought that we heard gunshots, so we paused for a while, listening for sirens and shouts. I have never doubted that we would have easily heard the Glenville shoot-out had we lived on this ridge in 1968.

In the restive 1968 summer, Glenville was on edge after waves of Civil Rights protests reacting to Reverend King's assassination swept through the city. At the time, Cleveland ranked among the ten largest and most influential cities in America, with thriving steel plants, a world-class orchestra, and Case Western Reserve University, a leading engineering and technology institution. It was the first major city to elect an African American mayor, Carl Stokes Jr. Because of its national profile, FBI and local police were spying on the nearly fifty Civil Rights and Black Nationalists groups active in the city. Commissions and historians never resolved how the shoot-out began on July 23, except they agree that Glenville resident Fred Ahmed Evans, leader of the Black Nationalists of New Libya, was at the center of the melee. Evans claimed he was ambushed by undercover officers with submachine guns, but local police accused his group of opening fire first. The protests, looting, and burning continued for days even after Evans was captured. He was convicted of first-degree murder for the seven people killed, including three police officers. The U.S. Supreme Court later reduced his capital punishment sentence to life in prison, and he died in custody ten years later.

I visited Glenville as a pilgrimage moment on a quiet morning long after the simmering summer of 1968. The drive to Glenville took me down Superior Avenue through East Cleveland, a jumble of shattered buildings and rubble-strewn lots that epitomized the way white flight gutted cities like Cleveland.[11] Marked out in 1853, Superior Avenue was designed to

---

[11] For background on the policies in the United States that segregate housing, disadvantage African Americans, and lead to urban decay, see Roithmayr, *Reproducing Racism*, and Rothstein, *Color of Law*.

funnel commercial traffic and personal travelers from the eastern bluffs above the city into downtown, tracing the watershed creeks toward Lake Erie's shore. I wound alongside Forest Hill Park, created from the estate of John D. Rockefeller after the turn of the twentieth century. My drive ended before the blocks along Superior Avenue improved, as further down it bisected Cleveland's grand Cultural Gardens adorning Martin Luther King Boulevard.

I drove through three miles of an American war zone, a war of the United States against its own African American citizens. I felt sickened—truly. The neighborhood was like Selma, proud Selma, and the Lower Ninth Ward. So much of the cityscape was broken, comprised of fire-damaged houses without windows as well as rutted, littered lawns behind fences of two-story public housing. I saw abandoned storefront churches, now boarded up, that were scattered among half-cleared lots and small car repair shops. Clusters of two or three men gathered in a desultory way on sidewalks and street corners. A few individuals waited at bus stops to get downtown while some pedestrians hurried to start their day, and cars zoomed through their neighborhood. Their purposefulness contrasted with shuttered businesses and empty Gospel ministries that flanked too many grassed-over or packed-dirt lots. I spied bright spots on side streets: a gracious house with a well-loved yard, a fruitful community garden, or a historic church that still welcomed worshippers in to praise God. These represented the hopeful anchors of possibility amidst desolation.

Literally nothing remained of the Glenville shoot-out. The businesses from that era had burned in the fiery aftermath of the clash. Even the famed but long-crumbling Esquire Hotel skeleton had finally been razed. A simple dirt footpath bisected the weedy lot, with no memorial to that fierce, tragic July battle. There was not even a simple gray marker on an aluminum pole like the one indicating the 1811 Woodland Plantation uprising in Louisiana. All that was left to chronicle Glenville's struggle for its share of America's opportunities was scattered debris, scars on sidewalks, and empty streets as cars sped by. I turned toward home, and I reflected upon the human suffering I had witnessed in my brief foray through Cleveland's scorned neighborhood. Glenville would be out of sight but not out of earshot and certainly not out of mind for me now.

A sobering realization tugged at my heart. More than a color line, I confronted a color wall that protected white status and white sensibilities in this country. How easy it was for Americans like me to be colorblind about the color line that runs through this country. White people did not travel to "Black neighborhoods," so they did not see the battlegrounds of the war against African Americans, as in Glenville. Such neighborhoods and schools were set apart by street boundaries and traffic patterns as effective as any ten-foot wall. Middle-class white people did not have to see the intersectional suffering of race with poor health, race with poor education, and race with poverty itself. I recognized how America's original sin ran along the line between Black and white in the country, not hidden but ostentatiously on display for anyone with eyes to see.

The next moment in Cleveland became my expedition into the names and public markings everywhere that tell us who counts and who does not. I needed to pay attention to the color line emblazoned on our streets. Walk with me on the bluffs through the neighborhoods east of Cleveland.

Moment 2: Northern White Resistance and the Lost Cause

In the liminal space between leaving Cleveland and reaching Cleveland Heights—in just a flash, really—I perceived the link between the Glenville shoot-out and a larger pattern of white resistance to racial equality in northern spaces. Northern white people did not have to confront their fears and prejudices about Black people or do much to assert their claims to superiority before the Civil War. However, with the waves of African

Americans moving north, threats to white racial supremacy became big problems for northern states. The reaction of whites in northern cities to the Great Migration explained so much about the structure of northern cities, the names and design of northern spaces, the fierce race battles of the 1960s, and the reckonings today. In this moment, I dug more deeply into evidence of whites resisting African American equality in something as seemingly innocuous as place names.

Before this color-line trek, when I heard "Jim Crow" I thought of the Deep South. I heard "the land of cotton," as the chillingly bright rhyme proclaimed, and thought of Georgia, Alabama, and Mississippi. I remembered the tufts of cotton snared in roadside weeds in "Bloody Lowndes" County in Alabama. I thought that I had left Dixie when I left Charlottesville decades ago. Dixie, with its Southern Cross flag, was far removed from the Midwest where I lived as an adult. Then, on a driving trip in the spring, I found myself speeding along South Dixie Highway with Confederate flags on porches—in Michigan.

Pilgrimage moments usually stop at holy shrines for peace or inspiration, but instead I stopped for the Dixie Highway. The transcontinental highway movement in this country exploded in the early twentieth century along with the mass production of cars. National civic boards sought to secure several continuous automobile and trucking routes from coast to coast, just like the transcontinental railway triumph. Unknowingly, I had for decades traveled along the earliest east-to-west highways. Most have been replaced by the Interstate Highway System, but their old names remain affixed to rusting rural route markers.[12] I discovered these three national high-

---

[12] Researchers have documented how the Interstate Highway System as planned and built plowed up African American city neighborhoods to smooth white flights out of cities, bisecting and destroying communities that have never recovered. See, e.g., Linda Poon, "The Racial Injustice of American Highways," *Bloomberg CityLab*, June 3, 2020, https://www.bloomberg.com/news/articles/2020-06-03/what-highways-mean-to-the-george-floyd-protesters.

ways: Lincoln Highway, a northern route named in 1913 that extended from New York Times Square to Lincoln Park in San Francisco; the Jefferson Davis Highway, conceived as a southern connecting route from Arlington, Virginia, to San Diego, California, also dedicated in 1913; and the Dixie Highway, launched in 1914 to connect Sault St. Marie on the Upper Peninsula of Michigan to Miami, Florida, by starting in Ohio and Kentucky and then heading southeast and northwest. A half century after the Emancipation Proclamation and the Thirteenth Amendment, five decades after slavery had been definitively outlawed in America, the United States dedicated two transnational highways to commemorate the Civil War and only one to the Union's triumph.

Lost Cause shrines were all around in public spaces in both the North and South, so I paused to consider how such shrines perpetuate racial injustice. The Lost Cause myths emerged in the late nineteenth century, after federal legislators from Confederate states stymied the Reconstruction.[13] The myth resurrected the rectitude of Southern slaveholding society by erecting statutes to Confederate civic and military leaders. The leaders were praised for their heroism and patriotism and for defending the "Southern way of life." At its core, the Lost Cause has distorted history by thrusting culpability for the war on Northern states, by framing secession with a freedom narrative, and by exonerating Confederate generals and soldiers for their military incompetencies. Most perniciously, the Lost Cause myth has always avoided explicit racial categories and covered up the fundamental Southern commitment to white supremacy and Black exploitation. Lost Cause propaganda spread throughout northern and southern states during the first half of twentieth century. Many people interpret the

---

[13] For background on the myth of the Lost Cause, see Clint Smith, "The War on Nostalgia: What Will It Take to End the Myth of the Lost Cause?," *Atlantic Magazine*, June 2021, 52–61.

Lost Cause ideology as a psychological enslavement of African Americans once their physical enslavement ended.

Civil War Lost Cause myths include such assertions as:

- The South seceded to protest Northern states' overreaching through federal government policies.

- Slavery was good for enslaved people.

- The Union only won the Civil War due to greater numbers, not because of better battle strategies and a more diversified, productive economy.

- Most Confederate soldiers were not slaveowners and did not care about maintaining slavery or white power.

- Robert E. Lee was a successful general, a hero, and a devout Christian.[14]

Some Lost Cause believers, such as the United Daughters of the Confederacy, promoted their agendas through explicit monument building. The Lost Cause also advanced by gaining full-throated zealots who denounced the "War of Northern Aggression," waving flags and singing "Dixie." Sometimes it advanced through unwitting influencers—like me. I recalled a conversation where I unintentionally joined the Lost Cause project. At eighteen, I visited my sister at the University of Virginia during her junior year. Sharing tidbits of her college life, she delightedly told me that her roommate was named Sumter after heroic Fort Sumter. "Wow!" I exclaimed, pretending I understood how remarkably courageous, noble, and patriotic Sumter's parents were. Actually, I knew nothing of Civil War history at the time; I didn't even know where Fort Sumter was. Now I know.

---

[14] See "The Lost Cause: Origins and Definition," *American Battlefield Trust*, accessed December 9, 2020, https://www.battlefields.org/learn/articles/lost-cause-definition-and-origins.

The very first Civil War battle was waged at Fort Sumter, now preserved as a national historic site. The southern troops captured the fort from the Union Army and defended it throughout the Civil War because of its strategic location in the Charleston Harbor. In 1932, the United Daughters of the Confederacy erected a bronze-and-granite memorial to the Confederate defenders from Charleston that read "Count them happy who for their faith and their courage endured a great fight." When I learned the history of Fort Sumter, I was ashamed of my unknowing celebration of the Confederate troops who had been falsely glorified as "enduring a great fight." Had I known, I should have pushed back. I might have pointed out that the so-called heroes of Fort Sumter chose to betray the United States. They chose to secede from the Union because they wanted to preserve the so-called Southern way of life. In the words of lawmakers at the secession convention in 1861, "Our [Confederate] position is thoroughly identified with the institution of slavery—the greatest material interest of the world."[15] More importantly, through my intellectual laziness and desire to get along, I condoned an ideology that held African Americans to be worthy of enslavement. That's how white complicity has failed people of color in this country. Although it was a single opportunity to reject racial oppression, I bungled it. Small things add up.

Yes, small things add up, but public monuments have been no small thing. The Lost Cause has been costly both in dollars and in its impact of erasing from white Americans' minds the centrality of slavery in the country's history. Researchers estimate that, during the decade between 2008 and 2018, over $40 million in public money was spent to maintain monuments

---

[15] A Mississippi lawmaker's speech, quoted in Smith, "War on Nostalgia," 58. While not all Confederate soldiers held slaves, all white citizens of secessionists states benefited from slavery, at least to the extent of enjoying moral and social superiority from a whole race of people declared lesser than themselves.

to the Confederacy.[16] I recollected the Confederate monument
on the Montgomery Capitol grounds and Jefferson Davis's
"white house" across the street. They were unapologetic and
well kept. The monuments validated Confederate ideology
because taxpayer money has always signified public support.
In the course of the national racial reckoning over the past year,
many Confederate monuments have tumbled; some have been
moved or reframed.[17] These are small, but significant steps.

Finding Dixie Highway in Michigan sent me on a holy quest
to find other Confederate remembrances in street names and
public monuments. I became intrigued by Lee Road and Monticello Boulevard, which intersect near my house. Lee is a major
artery running almost ten miles north–south through the eastern suburbs of Cleveland. Although it may be just another
American surname, Lee Road was marked out as a key thor-
oughfare in this region in the late nineteenth century. Probably
not a coincidence. Lee Road and Monticello Boulevard formed
the southeast boundary of the Forest Hill development, which
was planned in the 1950s with restrictive covenants in the
deeds that excluded non-whites and non-Christians.[18] Its major
transecting road was Mount Vernon Boulevard. For years, I

[16] Brian Palmer and Seth Freed Wessler, "The Costs of the Confederacy,"
Smithsonian Magazine, December 2018, https://www.smithsonianmag.com
/history/costs-confederacy-special-report-180970731/.

[17] Levar Stoney, the mayor of Richmond, recently wrote: "On live television,
we watched a 100-ton crane lift Stonewall Jackson from his pedestal. Cheers
erupted from hundreds who had gathered in the rain to witness its removal.
Like other residents in our city that day, I cried. Over the next week, contrac-
tors removed 14 pieces of Confederate iconography throughout the city. . . .
First erected in 1890, as part of a real estate development on the outskirts of
downtown, the actual purpose [of the Confederate monuments] was pure
Jim Crow—to put Black people in their place." See Stoney, "I Needed to Heal
My City. But I Needed to Apologize First," *New York Times*, May 22, 2021,
https://www.nytimes.com/2021/05/22/opinion/confederate-monuments
-richmond-levar-stoney.html.

[18] For a full discussion about how private real estate covenants and bank
lending practices linked with federal mortgage policies to segregate American
neighborhoods and exclude non-whites, see Rothstein, *Color of Law*.

enjoyed savoring Monticello Boulevard's connection to my childhood memories of Virginia. After my pilgrimage moments in Charlottesville, I could not help but wonder about the developers' choice of street names: Monticello and Mount Vernon. These were the eighteenth-century plantations of Thomas Jefferson and George Washington that were managed through the conscripted labor of Black men, women, and children. Surely the street names encoded a message about who belonged in this lovely neighborhood and who did not.

I linked these street signs with other revelatory moments in Louisiana—*enslaved people* on the Whitney Plantation, not slaves; *freedom fighters* in 1811, not mutinous rebels. Because labels are so ubiquitous, so commonplace, they blend in. But names are not just names. They indoctrinate and persuade. Names matter. Signs matter, symbols matter, language matters. Moreover, there was a pattern and method to the naming incidents in my hometown and further afield. Naming initiatives adopted in northern cities during the twentieth century ensconced white resistance to the equality of African Americans.

With the grace of *Shema!*, I began to see America's original sin in the form of white resistance to racial justice displayed on signs and symbols all around. Once seen, I could not unsee it, as the expression goes. But the Lost Cause has been lost. In contrast to the legacies of America's racist past, in the next moment I counted small events that showed America was moving toward greater justice. They were small events, just beads of hope. Walk with me to count the beads of hope.

Moment 3: Counting Beads of Hope

Christ's command to his disciples was to pay attention, to keep eyes and ears open to experience God's Spirit moving in the world. In this moment, attending to the Spirit, I counted many moments of hope. I searched out bright spots where the work of justice was proceeding with slow, steady steps. I counted these moments, like praying a rosary, because small moments add up. More than that, counting beads of hope in prayer softened my heart to love a little more generously and sharpened my desire to find the good path. Beads of hope.

In my own family's travels, a collection of four small moments lined up allowed me to trace justice changes that had already been happening in America. First, in the late 1980s, complete strangers in our Bucks County, Pennsylvania, enclave would start up conversations with me: "Oh, your children have such beautiful tan skin. I love to touch their hair! What are they?" I bristled at their boldness claiming the right to touch my babies. I heard stereotypes embedded in their cheerful words and in their shallow compliments—a desire for me to see them as "good white people." Still, they could not resist their urge to assign my children to a low rung, a not-white station on America's racial caste hierarchy. Then, a decade later in Vermont, the questioning continued with a subtle shift. While adults refrained from interrogating us as their peers, our children bore the community's racial scrutiny. A child at the Catholic school in Burlington quizzed our second-grade daughter: "Why is your skin so dark?" The not-so-hidden presumption of "dark equals bad" was so stark and stinging that she cried in shame to repeat the words. But things shifted again with another decade and in another place—Cleveland Heights—more accustomed to a wide variety of skin and hair. My niece, who like her cousins is mixed race, related her kindergarten classmate's curiosity: "Why is your daddy brown and your mommy clear?" A fair question, well framed. Finally, not long ago, I walked the streets of the Noble neighborhood in Cleveland Heights. It had been integrated for decades. I greeted a young African American father as he raked fallen yellow leaves from the sidewalk. When his son asked who I was, the man simply said, "She's a neighbor." Like the question in the book of Joshua: What did these moments mean? To me they were four hopeful beads that I could count on and hold on to while dreaming that America might overcome the shackles of its past for the generations to come.

I also counted a bead of hope in the secret story of the "Oak Ridge 85" in Tennessee.[19] Eighty-five African American students from the Scarboro community enrolled in all-white Oak Ridge High School in the fall of 1955. Oak Ridge was not an incorporated city in Tennessee but a school district controlled by the U.S. Atomic Energy Commission. The Oak Ridge and Scarboro communities were "secret" since the Oak Ridge laboratories worked on the Manhattan Project. Black residents, who provided services to the professional scientists and their families, lived segregated from white residents in "hutments" in the Scarboro enclave. In a small wooded area, the huts offered meager fourteen-by-fourteen-foot shelters without plumbing or centralized heating for Black families. Scarboro had no school, although some children were bused to adjacent county districts. In 1955, with authority from President Eisenhower, African American students enrolled in Oak Ridge Junior High and High Schools, a plan firmly supported by the principal and teachers. Despite inevitable friction, the integration proceeded smoothly overall. Most noteworthy about Oak Ridge was the widespread conviction of both African American and white residents that their individual choices were necessary and just. Their actions were grounded in hope. I have counted the eighty-five students who integrated Oak Ridge High School and their classmates as beads of hope.

Spring Hill College in Mobile, Alabama, offered me another bead of hope to count.[20] The Jesuit-sponsored institution had a proud history of Civil Rights activism in the 1950s. That history included its participation in boycotts, its public advocacy,

[19] See Yvonne Thomas and Elizabeth Sims, "The Secret in Scarboro: The Oak Ridge 85," *WBIR.com*, accessed February 8, 2021, https://www.wbir.com/article/news/history/the-secret-in-scarboro-the-oak-ridge-85/51-2a202693-2ac8-4318-b162-10ef5e43972c.

[20] Erica Powell, "Race, Politics, and Progress: Spring Hill College in the Long Sixties," *Pax: Spring Hill College's Peace and Justice Magazine*, May 3, 2016, http://pax.shc.edu/story/race-politics-and-progress-spring-hill-college-long-sixties.

and its program of inviting Civil Rights leaders to campus. The college's first nine African American students enrolled in residential classes in 1954 in a quiet move managed directly by the president and a sociology professor, both Jesuits. College histories have recorded a remarkable night in 1957. Spring Hill students crept out from their dorms to chase away KKK members and stop them from burning a cross on the college lawn. By the end of the 1960s, all of the college's activities and units had been desegregated. In "Letter from a Birmingham Jail," Martin Luther King mentioned specifically the courage of Catholic leaders at Spring Hill College. A bead of hope.

I tallied stories along this pilgrimage that gave me hope. I savored them and prayed about them as beads of hope on a rosary. These were small moments, beads to count on the right side of history: like the women and men who fought their enslavement over centuries with every ounce of their being, like Venerable Henriette Delille who established schools and hospitals for people of color, like the Carver Project residents in Selma who cared for Bloody Sunday marchers, and like the faithful Edmundite Community feeding Selma's residents today. They showed me that justice proceeds day by day, moment by moment. Individual choices add up. That was King's message about the moral arc of the universe—it is long, but people's actions are bending it toward justice.

To wrap up this moment, I grabbed my shillelagh and secured a rosary to its handle. The rosary on the smooth, black handle reminded me to look for signs of justice. Walk with me and pay attention as I recount the story of how Cleveland Heights resisted segregation.[21] Those neighbors were also beads of hope.

---

[21] I use this powerful phrase as a grateful tribute to my neighbor's labor of love retelling our town's heroic deeds fifty years ago: Susan Kaeser, *Resisting Segregation: Cleveland Heights Activists Shape Their Community, 1964–1976* (Cleveland, OH: Cleveland Landmarks Press, 2020).

Moment 4: Resisting Segregation—Now

When I set off recollecting America's original sin, I never suspected that my path through the wilderness of race would lead me home. I had visited shrines and sights on the pilgrimage as moments in the story of oppression and discrimination in the United States, but I struggled with how to respond to what I experienced.[22] There was a gap in my understanding between what had happened in heroic moments and how these moments should shape my actions. My search to find holy signposts for just action, models that I might emulate, led me back to where I started. In my own hometown, I found signposts of racial justice in the form of resistance to segregation.[23] I followed their story by comparing what Cleveland Heights was "now" in 2020 with neighbors' actions "then" when they struggled to integrate the city's neighborhoods. Two moments, one powerful bead of hope.

Cleveland Heights perches on an eastern bluff above Cleveland's University Circle, home to hospitals, museums, public gardens and parks, and a wide array of social service organizations. In the early twentieth century, it was a streetcar suburb for families who could move outside the grimy industrial

---

[22] See above at "First Week: On the Threshold of a Journey," Moment 1: Reckoning, quoting from Paul Elie, *The Life You Save May Be Your Own: An American Pilgrimage* (New York: Macmillan Press, 2004), x.

[23] Many sociologists have written about the successes and failures of school integration, especially its impact on educational quality and student learning, neighborhood stabilization, and community well-being. See, e.g., Leonard Steinhorn and Barbara Diggs-Brown, *By the Color of Our Skin: The Illusion of Integration and the Reality of Race* (New York: A Dutton Book, 1999), especially the afterword about Shaker Heights, Ohio; John B. Diamond, "Still Separate and Unequal: Examining Race, Opportunity, and School Achievement in 'Integrated' Suburbs," *The Journal of Negro Education* (2006): 495–505; and George C. Galster, "White Flight from Racially Integrated Neighborhoods in the 1970s: The Cleveland Experience," *Urban Studies* 27, no. 3 (1990): 385–99, which suggests that neither Cleveland Heights's nor Shaker Heights's concerted work on integration was able to slow white flight after a tipping point of 20–50 percent of Black residential saturation was reached.

neighborhoods of central Cleveland. Gracious, tree-lined streets offered sites with imposing homes for the barons of Cleveland's industrial empires. There were also modest neighborhoods for people with more modest incomes. The population in the town tripled from 1920 to 1930 to 50,000 residents as streets were laid out and housing lots subdivided. Its growth slowed after 1950 and then started to decline in 1980, as the city's numbers seemed to reach a tipping point of 15 percent or more African Americans.

People have called the town gritty and liberal, or declining and dangerous, depending on their political persuasions. The conclusion some demographers have drawn from its numbers is that Cleveland Heights did not staunch white flight. But whiteness ought not be the measure of community value. By 2020, the city was a patchwork of middle- and working-class homes interspersed with mom-and-pop businesses and small apartment buildings along main avenues. Some districts were quite wealthy and some were not. Some were crime free and others not. Coyotes and deer could still shelter in the woods and ravines of the many large public parks and green spaces. The ethnicity of the residents has changed, but housing values have held steady. The municipal government has continually planned for new shopping and housing developments, as the city updated and refurbished itself to meet residents' need. Cleveland Heights has proved that stable neighborhoods welcome residents of all ancestries.

In the Cleveland Heights "now" moment, I walked through four "shrines of resistance," all within a couple of square miles in the northwest corner of Cleveland Heights. This area was the first to be settled and the first to be desegregated. With a pilgrim's fresh eyes, I saw each shrine as curious and startling in its own way. They all bore the costs of past struggles to resist segregation and white flight. It took some time to recognize them for the signposts that they were.

First, I visited the neighborhood of Forest Hill. On foot, I paced along the blocks of homes that chronicled the town's

demographic journey over the past half century. The neighborhood, designed on land once owned by the Rockefeller family,
straddled the municipal boundaries of Cleveland Heights, East
Cleveland, and Cleveland. It started as a desirable development for aspiring white middle-class families in the 1950s. The
mix of brick ranch houses and Normandy Tudor homes testified to the designers' vision for a cohesive, family-friendly
community that bordered on the enormous acreage of Forest
Hill Park. Public tennis courts and the small private swim club
completed the good life here. By 2020, Forest Hill's restrictive
covenants had long been abandoned, as a majority of white
residents ceded ownership to African Americans moving from
Cleveland in the 1980s. As I sauntered along the streets, decline
and instability radiated from weedy yards and peeling paint.
Not all houses (but many of them) showed signs of decay. I also
watched drivers navigate potholes and patched pavement
plaguing the gracefully curved boulevards. Some observers
would attribute the decline to the color of the residents' skin,
but I thought that Forest Hill, like Selma, was paying the price
for its Civil Rights courage.[24]

The second shrine that I toured was the Severance Mall and
the municipal service buildings situated nearby. In its prime
in the early 1970s, Severance, a collection of shops connected
by covered walkways to departments stores, had set the pace
for American retail. Recollecting the roll call of store brands
from its five decades felt to me like a funeral dirge for retail
across America. With each passing era, Severance has dropped

---

[24] The pattern of decline is a well-documented social, economic, and political problem. When Black families move into white neighborhoods, pan-
icked white homeowners flee, selling their homes at a loss and driving down
property values. As this cycle proceeds, tax revenues decline and municipal
investment decreases by policy or due to shrinking budgets. Mortgages and
loans for housing stock decline, so owners subdivide their living spaces to
make ends meet. More people, fewer city services, and declining income with
declining commercial opportunities together create a vicious cycle that re-
produces racism. See Roithmayr, *Reproducing Racism.*

closer to bankruptcy, moving from a conglomeration of high-end department stores to a collection of empty caverns. The clientele more recently has been too poor to support the movie theater, Walmart, or IHOP any longer. The principal retail anchors have no longer been upscale department stores but Home Depot and Dave's Market, where customers arrive by wheelchairs, buses, or on foot with grocery carriers dragged behind. On a Saturday morning, I ambled along the inner road encircling the central mall. I walked past a small but busy community hospital, the Christ Culture Church with tented worship for COVID times, and a dated post office. The drive-through banks, specialty clothing shops, and fast-food restaurants that I remembered from years past had all fled. Some outbuildings were shuttered; others had been demolished and the land allowed to go fallow.

On the north side of the mall property, I pondered the Cleveland Heights City Hall complex. It housed the police station, the jail, and the mayor's office. Apartments dedicated to Section 8 housing were sited along the western edge of the complex. I knew that in the 1950s, across busy Mayfield Avenue from Severance, the Jewish Community Center used to welcome families for recreation and social events. As many Jewish residents moved further east to more rural areas away from Cleveland, the JCC relocated itself as well. The land was redeveloped for cluster homes, inviting investment by health care professionals who worked in University Circle down the hill. Looking from City Hall to the old JCC property, I gazed upon a complex of senior and low-income housing; the city's fire and rescue station, whose sirens blared through the night; and the Lutheran high school's pitted cinder track. The waves of development represented decades of resisting white flight in a repeated rebalancing of neighbors, needs, and revenue.

The third shrine was the multifaceted Jewish community in Cleveland Heights. With the initial wave of Jewish residents moving out of Cleveland-Glenville in the first half of the twentieth century, two massive temple campuses were sited just a mile outside the Cleveland border. B'nai Jeshrun Temple, known as the Temple on the Heights, was a thriving worship and community space for six decades until it relocated further east, further from Cleveland's browning populations. A Christian gospel church later transformed the space for large praise gatherings and fellowship, renaming it "The Civic." In a similar pattern, the Park Synagogue campus moved into Cleveland Heights at the height of the Glenville exodus in 1950. It boasted a Frank Lloyd Wright–styled domed worship hall, a day school, and a preschool. The Park Synagogue recently built a new campus, again, further away from Cleveland at the eastern edge of the county, and it just announced that it would close the Heights campus. Another exodus.

In contrast, a Hasidic Orthodox Jewish community has called Cleveland Heights home for decades. On Friday evenings and Saturday mornings, I have driven carefully past large families walking from close-by houses to temples along Lee Road. Old men, and young men too, sport traditional white with black prayer shawls and wide-brimmed black hats at jaunty angles. Their wives are protected from prying gazes in their modest calf-length skirts and hair concealed under wigs or scarves. Some children hold their parents' hands for safety, while others skip along anticipating friends at Sabbath services. Butcher shops and yeshivas are always shuttered for the holy day but open on Sunday mornings. Feeling the weight of my difference, I have never entered these shops in all the years I've passed by them. Whenever I have walked along blocks behind the synagogues, very few neighbors have returned my greetings. More often, wary glances or harsh frowns have met my tentative efforts to connect with the families who live so close to me. The Hasidic community was part of Cleveland Heights yet it held itself apart.

The fourth shrine was actually a collection of shrines, literally.[25] At every corner, along every major block, everywhere

[25] Marian J. Morton, *Cleveland Heights Congregations* (Mount Pleasant, SC: Arcadia Publishing, 2009).

I stepped, it seemed like I stumbled upon a Christian church. If America was experiencing the rise of the "nones," no one had told Cleveland Heights. Most of the dozen or so churches have remained active since the 1970s, although they are thinning and graying, like their congregants. I could have had my pick of nearly any denomination within a half mile of the Mayfield-Taylor intersection. I passed the Greek Orthodox cathedral, which welcomed guests for the August fish fries. There were several full gospel temples and fellowships for Christian praise. Multiple Presbyterian churches divided by demographics and worship styles (Black, mixed, or mostly white) tried to entice me with progressive sermons and community education. The Disciples of Christ was a small but mighty congregation. It hosted the local emergency food pantry that was a lifeline for pandemic-stricken families this past year. Unfortunately, St. Louis Church, the Catholic parish for the neighborhood, had closed in 2010, but the sisters' convent adjacent to it seemed to show activity whenever I walked by. In these congregations' halls in past decades, neighbors met for the good of the community to plan and strategize, to hear concerns and resolve differences. Most importantly, they took seriously the dictates of their faith to live justly.

These four shrines held the key to Cleveland Heights's efforts to respond justly to the Civil Rights Movement and the challenge of racial integration. Outsiders ask whether Cleveland Heights is "safe." While they may see economic decline and demographic challenges, I see neighbors. Images of the Glenville shoot-out contrasted in my mind with contemporary events in the past reckoning year. Last spring, our family joined the stream of citizens heading for the City Hall Plaza to protest George Floyd's killing. In other cities, protests led to violence. In our town, residents mingled with police officers and community leaders. We chanted that Black lives matter, and we knelt in silence for eight minutes and forty-six seconds. The silence honoring Mr. Floyd was a moment of justice so characteristic of Cleveland Heights. Its already-but-not-yet struggle for racial justice was built, layer by layer, upon a firm foundation laid down in the 1960s and '70s when a handful of community leaders changed the fate of people in this small city.

The next moment of "resisting segregation—then" led me to that momentous time decades ago. Neighbors heard neighbors' cries for justice, and together they linked arms to create a city where all people would be welcome. *Shema!*

Moment 5: Resisting Segregation—Then

Cleveland Heights neighbors' decision to resist white flight and to promote integration developed through an intentional coalition of Black and white citizens.[26] A courageous project led by the local Catholic parish also proved vital to their success. These were beads-of-hope moments. I recollected them and tallied them as signposts of justice, as moments of "plenty good trouble."

Residents of Cleveland Heights were excruciatingly aware of East Cleveland's fate in the 1960s. Black families moving out of Glenville into the nearby suburbs set off a predictable pattern. White families fled as real-estate brokers "busted blocks." White residents feared declining property values, dangerous streets, and deteriorating schools. Their fears were self-fulfilling when they fled in panic to suburbs even further from urban populations of African Americans. The integration of a street, even the sale of a single house, sparked a frenzied exodus of stable middle-class families. A cascade of economic and social crises followed in the wake of such reckless flight. In the matter of a decade or so, East Cleveland became one of the most segregated and poorest cities in Ohio. It collapsed under the weight of its residents' fear.

[26] Kaeser, *Resisting Segregation*, and Marian J. Morton, *Cleveland Heights: The Making of an Urban Suburb* (Mount Pleasant, SC: Arcadia Publishing, 2002).

Cleveland Heights citizens chose to walk a different path on the delicate color-line journey to city-wide integration. The violent death of a young local pastor during a 1964 demonstration against segregated schools in Cleveland-Glenville galvanized Cleveland Heights. Residents hoped to find a path forward that was more peaceful, more constructive, and more lasting by building cooperation among neighbors across the color line. What distinguished Cleveland Heights was the clarity of its purpose—to resettle African Americans in the town deliberately.[27] The integration plan depended upon a cooperating pair of citizens' committees: the Committee to Improve Community Relations (CICR, African American led) and the Heights Citizens for Human Rights committee (HCHR, white led). A short list of their activities showed the scope of their work:

- lobbying state and local governments to formulate Fair Housing laws and outlaw racial steering;

- lobbying the school district for human relations policies to diversify faculty and staff to meet the needs of African American children;

- coordinating "living room" conversations among neighbors about race at the rate of several dozen each year;

- recruiting local churches for education groups and social action committees; and

- organizing frequent protest marches with plenty of publicity.[28]

Another vital plank of the plan focused specifically on supporting Black families who wanted to move to Cleveland Heights. To help them find housing, HCHR identified homeowners who were willing to sell on an open market, without

[27] Kaeser, *Resisting Segregation*, 46–71.
[28] Kaeser, passim.

racial steering. Then, with financial backing from local churches, they created a fund for mortgage assistance and housing repair. This addressed the problem that African Americans were routinely denied federally secured mortgages and equity loans. Finally, CICR worked with schools to ease Black children's transition into mostly white classrooms. Not all the work went on peacefully. In the decade between 1963 and 1973, segregationists bombed and vandalized the houses of over twenty-five residents, Black and white, trying to stymie the integration of the city. But in the main, Cleveland Heights citizens' efforts avoided the white flight and massive collapse that East Cleveland had experienced.

St. Ann Church, now Communion of Saints, joined the fight to integrate Cleveland Heights.[29] Hundreds of times I have walked by the church pediment proclaiming *Haec Est Domus Deo* ("This is the House of God"), but the inscription took on a new meaning for me. The Catholic Church in the U.S. has often been criticized for the failure to use its moral authority to promote racial justice,[30] but local dioceses and parishes tell a different story. Decades ago, St. Ann's pastor and parishioners initiated an audit of local realtors to find extensive evidence of racial steering, which made all the difference to this town.

---

[29] Kaeser, 164–75 and passim.

[30] The United States Conference of Catholic Bishops has issued only two major pastoral letters against racism: Brothers and Sisters to Us (1979) and, forty years later, Open Wide Our Hearts (2018). Both can be found at the USCCB's website: https://www.usccb.org/committees/african-american -affairs. See also Alison Mearns Benders, *Reading, Praying, Living The US Bishops' Open Wide Our Hearts: A Faith Formation Guide* (Collegeville, MN: Liturgical Press, 2020). Rightly, Black and white Catholics have noted the U.S. bishops' silence and halting steps. See, e.g., Olga Segura, *Birth of a Movement: Black Lives Matter and the Catholic Church* (Maryknoll, NY: Orbis, 2021), which relates some of the church's history with civil rights; and Bryan Massingale, *Racism and the Catholic Church* (Maryknoll, NY: Orbis Press, 2014). Regarding white Christianity's failure to address racial oppression, see, e.g., Robert P. Jones, *White Too Long: The Legacy of White Supremacy in American Christianity* (New York: Simon & Schuster, 2020).

The audit grew out of the Diocese of Cleveland Commission on Catholic Community Action, which in turn was a direct response to *Gaudium et Spes* and the Second Vatican Council. In 1969, the commission called for Cleveland Catholics to respond immediately and urgently to social issues, including housing, poverty, health, and employment. The diocese created a plan for parishes to study racism and then asked them to create specific community responses. The commission also established the Action for Change fund to help parishes execute their projects. Answering the call, St. Ann formed the Social Action Housing Committee in 1971 to audit real estate offices in Shaker Heights and Cleveland Heights.

Over the course of several months, the committee sent volunteers posing as buyers into real estate offices in the area. Matched pairs of buyers, a Black couple and a white couple with similar backgrounds, recorded how they were treated as they requested tours of houses and neighborhoods. A comprehensive report documented multiple serious violations of federal housing laws at all local firms. Rather than choosing litigation, the committee worked with municipal law directors on a best-practice model to encourage realtors to work for fair housing. While some businesses were angered and some parishioners disliked the dissent that the project engendered, the report received public support and impacted real estate sales practices across Cuyahoga County. St. Ann's project generated national attention from communities wishing to integrate. It also resulted in the formation of a permanent interfaith committee for fair housing in Cleveland Heights.

The story of America's original sin has played out in every village and city across the country. But Cleveland Heights neighbors became another signpost for me, another moment of "plenty good work" in the struggle to build racially just communities. The heart of their witness was human relationships, just as I had discovered over and over with other witnesses on this journey. The successful integration of Cleveland Heights depended upon all members of the community with different and complementary identities working together for a shared future. Their goals were not framed by charity, guilt, rights, or demands. Their goals were framed by justice, neighborly justice. Although the citizens committees may not have used the phrase "prophetic imagination," in fact they imagined a different possible future and took concrete steps to make it true. Just as importantly, Cleveland Heights demonstrated what would happen when even a small group of individuals seized the moment. Every moment of our lives presents a chaos-kairos-creation opportunity for us to choose justice. The 1960s presented a few individuals in a small town the opportunity to create a more just world. In that moment, they said yes.

The closing moments of this race and grace pilgrimage presented me with a just reckoning. The Shema's closing commandment rang out in my mind, as if Jesus were speaking to me: "*You* shall love your neighbor as yourself." I took the next moment to collect the fruits of this pilgrimage so that I could sort out my response to the reckonings that I had seen challenging this nation.

Moment 6: Just Reckonings

Reckonings call for a response. Just reckonings call for a just response. After recollecting America's original sin from its founding until now, from Charlottesville to Cleveland, this moment was about response.

A recent family moment made the reckonings urgent and personal. Last Christmas Eve, our family was enjoying dinner all together—kids, grandchildren, partners, and spouses. The doorbell rang and a sharp knock quickly followed. We saw the flashing lights of a police cruiser through the front window. When my husband rose to answer the door, thoughts of Black men killed by police made my heart race. Thankfully, the episode ended calmly and quickly. The police were checking about a neighbor's report that a Black man had stolen a package from our porch. That "Black man" was my husband, collecting a package from his own front door. The neighbor who reported this knew who we were; that neighbor had eaten at our table and traded stories with us in the driveway. I shook my head, incredulous but still shivering with relief. For other Black men, such encounters have ended in violence.

Personal and national moments of reckoning called me to take stock of what stopped me from working more authentically on racial justice and how to step up. After all, the point of a pilgrimage is to encounter God in the wilderness and return to daily life changed because of the holy encounters. If this time-apart pilgrimage was to be more than spiritual tourism, I had to gather the gleanings and commit to living according to the wisdom given to me. Some gleanings were more obvious than others, but that did not make them less true or less urgent. Together they showed me the need for a prophetic imagination that would align what I believed in with what I chose to do.[31]

Here are gleanings of wisdom that I gathered on this race and grace pilgrimage:

A first gleaning—social imagination: Social imagination means connecting our individual experiences with the experiences of others through empathy. I learned from nearly all pilgrimage moments that a major factor in perpetuating racial oppression today was white indifference to and studied ignorance about ongoing racism. That was not new, but my travels revealed how complex and tangled America's story of race was and how it is alive and vicious in all of our lives. My sin was in shielding myself from painful experiences and the suffering around me. In response, I have committed to listening, engaging, and learning to cultivate a deeper, more empathetic understanding of racism beginning with human relationships and social imagination.

---

[31] Segura, *Birth of a Movement*, 58: "We can use the resources of our faith to enter into an activist space using the doctrine and words of Jesus. White church leaders and Catholics can create a church where the oppressed can truly heal and be free, where they can truly repent and, eventually, stand in true allyship."

A second gleaning—cultural imagination: I learned that beyond individual sins, people of color continue to be exploited and violated. Cultural imagination means connecting individual experiences with the humanly created structures, values and ideas that shape people's lives together. Systems have been designed to advance white interests and place the costs on people who are not white. My sin here was not for the past structures but for my current responses. I have committed to being more authentic in my own values and habits. I have committed to supporting organizations and initiatives designed to change systems and structures, especially those that aim to change how we value human beings.

A third gleaning—prophetic imagination: I learned from the courage and decisiveness of signpost witnesses who acted for justice when and how they could within their own spheres of responsibility. Prophetic imagination calls people to envision a shared future that is more than just the community we now have and to work for that vision. My sin here has been a failure to see how justice must explicitly govern every choice I make, both professional and personal. I have committed to exercising a prophetic imagination by following the witnesses I met on this pilgrimage. The path to racial justice will have to include halting ongoing harms, preventing further injustices, remedying the past wounds, and creating a shared future that has not yet been.

A fourth gleaning—hope: I learned about the precarious balance of urgency and deliberateness when cultivating justice. America's sin and individual sins against Black Americans and people of color were seeded in the founding of this nation. The deep-rooted vine of injustice has choked people's lives in every era of the nation's history. The demand for justice has always been urgent. However, deep change takes time, as when we touch individuals' hearts, rewrite institutional and governmental policies, and convert the culture in which we live. The parable of the sower and the parable of the fig tree offered me hope. The parables use the metaphors of growth and emergence to point out God's active grace. Seeds landing on good ground, when cultivated with fertilizer, water, and weeding, will bring forth a rich harvest. I have committed to hope in God's promise of emancipation, in Christ's already-with-us redemption, and in the Spirit's winds of change stirring again in a kairos dawn.

With these gleanings held close in my heart, I spent much of this moment pacing and praying. "When you pray, move your feet." I prayed about the reckonings that I had put aside when I entered the wilderness of this journey. I prayed for all the suffering I had seen, then and now. I prayed for forgiveness. I hoped and prayed that I would not be ashamed to yearn for justice and would not forget my commitments vowed in this moment. I prayed for grace for this nation and its people. But I knew that words can be easy grace. Living into the transformation that I experienced on pilgrimage meant returning now to the responsibilities entrusted to my care. I paced into the final moment of this color-line gift of grace. More than ever, I heard the Spirit call: "*Shema!* Pay attention and respond!"

Moment 7: On That Day

Like every sore-footed, weary-legged pilgrim, I anticipated eagerly and regretted apprehensively my reunion with the world. This pilgrimage started a year ago when the country's reckonings broke my heart and summoned me—both. I could not turn away. I had to pay attention to the triple reckonings of our nation. I had to *Shema!* The racial reckonings drove me into the wilderness to find a still center of hope in the whirlwind of our times.

In the liminal time of this race and grace journey, so much happened, yet things were still the same. Here's what happened: I was chagrined at the suffering and tragedy of slavery. I was chastised and convicted by the way my white life has advanced at the cost of Black Americans' expense. I became convinced that racial injustice remained a yet-intractable fact of American life, still distributing benefits and costs unjustly. Along the way, I prayed for God's grace to see with open eyes. I hoped for—and found—wise companions in the struggle for justice. I discovered possibilities for a more just future.

Now, the recollection of America's original sin has brought me full circle. I started planning this pilgrimage in the reckoning days of Black Lives Matter protests just after George Floyd's killing. I paced and prayed my way through a year, a full cycle to the promising moment of Pentecost Sunday. With Pentecost, the church celebrates the Spirit's outpouring of grace into human hearts. My reentry into daily life coincided with Pentecost, the moment when the Holy Spirit descended upon Christ's disciples to fill them with passion and hope for the mission he entrusted to them. Before the Spirit filled them with fire and grace, they huddled in the upper room. They waited in a liminal time and space neither here nor there. They waited on God. Then the Spirit churned their hearts. Holy wisdom ignited their imaginations and strengthened their resolve. Pentecost flames stirred them with the reality of Christ's resurrection. They rushed out to create their world in the image of Christ.

The invitation to create our world according to God's just love is as urgent in our day as it has always been in human history. One and all, we are summoned to create the just community that our country has promised but has never yet achieved. Listen and respond! *Shema!*

"[G]ive, and it will be given to you. A good measure, pressed down, shaken together and running over, will be poured into your lap; for the measure you give will be the measure you get back."

Luke 6:38

The day of racial justice in America remains a future promise. I know that the day will arrive only when we bestow a great and generous love upon each other as one community in Christ. I try to imagine what a healed nation will look like, when we live into the promised land that beckons us.

On that day, the nation will live into its founding promise that "all people are created equal."

On that day, shackled limbs will be healed and shackled lives will be free.

On that day, all the tears we have shed—all of them—will be wiped away.

On that day, we shall live as neighbors together in the promised land of our loving God.

On that day, we will live as gift to one another.

On that day, we will tell our children how we made it over.

How long until that day? It depends upon our faithfulness to justice. We hasten that day, not long now, when we grab our walking sticks, cling to our prayers of contrition and hope, carry each other's crosses, and follow the signpost witnesses who show us the way.

Walk with me! *Shema!*

Selected Bibliography

Baptist, Edward E. *The Half Has Never Been Told: Slavery and the Making of American Capitalism.* New York: Basic Books, 2016.

Belenky, Mary Field, Blythe McVicker Clinchy, Nancy Rule Goldberger, and Jill Mattuck Tarule. *Women's Ways of Knowing: The Development of Self, Voice, and Mind.* New York: Basic Books, 1986.

Benders, Alison Mearns. *Just Prayer: A Book of Hours for Peacemakers and Justice Seekers.* Collegeville, MN: Liturgical Press, 2015.

Benders, Alison Mearns. *Reading, Praying, Living the US Bishops' Open Wide Our Hearts: A Faith Formation Guide.* Collegeville, MN: Liturgical Press, 2020.

Bennett, Lerone. *Before the Mayflower: A History of the Negro in America 1619–1964.* Rev. ed. London: Penguin Books, 1970.

Blight, David W. *Frederick Douglass: Prophet of Freedom.* New York: Simon & Schuster, 2020.

Blum, Edward J., and Paul Harvey. *The Color of Christ: The Son of God and the Saga of Race in America.* Chapel Hill, NC: UNC Press Books, 2012.

Boadt, Lawrence, Richard J. Clifford, and Daniel J. Harrington. *Reading the Old Testament: An Introduction.* Mahwah, NJ: Paulist Press, 2012.

Bonilla-Silva, Eduardo. *Racism without Racists: Color-Blind Racism and the Persistence of Racial Inequality in the United States.* Washington, D.C.: Rowman & Littlefield, 2006.

Bridges, Flora Wilson. *Resurrection Song: African-American Spirituality.* New York: Orbis Press, 2001.

Brueggemann, Walter. *The Land Overtures to Biblical Theology.* Rev. ed. Minneapolis: Fortress Press, 2002.

Brueggemann, Walter. *Materiality as Resistance: Five Elements for Moral Action in the Real World*. Louisville, KY: John Knox Press, 2020.

Brueggemann, Walter. *Prophetic Imagination*. Rev. ed. Minneapolis: Fortress Press, 1978.

Brueggemann, Walter. *Tenacious Solidarity: Biblical Provocations on Race, Religion, Climate, and the Economy*. Edited by Davis Hankins. Minneapolis: Fortress Press, 2018.

Clark, Emily, and Virginia Meacham Gould. "The Feminine Fact of Afro-Catholicism in New Orleans, 1727–1852." *The William and Mary Quarterly* 59, no. 2 (April 2002): 409–48.

Cone, James. *The Cross and the Lynching Tree*. New York: Orbis Press, 2011.

Copeland, M. Shawn. "Blackness Past, Blackness Future—and Theology." *South Atlantic Quarterly* 112, no. 4 (2013): 625–40.

Copeland, M. Shawn. *Enfleshing Freedom: Body, Race, and Human Being*. Minneapolis: Fortress Press, 2010.

Copeland, M. Shawn. *Knowing Christ Crucified: The Witness of African American Religious Experience*. New York: Orbis Press, 2018.

Copeland, M. Shawn. *The Subversive Power of Love: The Vision of Henriette Delille*. Mahwah, NJ: Paulist Press, 2009.

Copeland, M. Shawn, LaReine-Marie Mosely, and Albert J. Raboteau, eds. *Uncommon Faithfulness: The Black Catholic Experience*. New York: Orbis Press, 2009.

Crenshaw, Kimberlé Williams, ed. *Seeing Race Again: Countering Colorblindness across the Disciplines*. Berkeley, CA: University of California Press, 2019.

Davis, Cyprian. *The History of Black Catholics in the United States*. Chestnut Ridge, NY: Crossroads Press, 1990.

Davis, Cyprian, and Jamie Phelps, eds. *Stamped with the Image of God: African Americans as God's Image in Black*. New York: Orbis Press, 2003.

Delgado, Richard, and Jean Stefancic. *Critical Race Theory: An Introduction*. Vol. 20. New York: NYU Press, 2017.

DiAngelo, Robin. *White Fragility: Why It's So Hard for White People to Talk about Racism*. Boston, MA: Beacon Press, 2018.

Dorrien, Gary J. *Breaking White Supremacy: Martin Luther King Jr. and the Black Social Gospel.* New Haven, CT: Yale University Press, 2018.

Dorrien, Gary J. *Reconstructing the Common Good: Theology and the Social Order.* Eugene, OR: Wipf and Stock Publishers, 1990.

Elie, Paul. *The Life You Save May Be Your Own: An American Pilgrimage.* New York: Macmillan, 2004.

Gates, Louis Henry, Jr. *The Black Church: This Is Our Story, This Is Our Song.* London: Penguin, 2021.

Gaustad, Edwin, and Leigh Schmidt. *The Religious History of America: The Heart of the American Story from Colonial Times to Today.* San Francisco, CA: HarperOne, 2004.

Glaude, Eddie S., Jr. *Begin Again: James Baldwin's America and Its Urgent Lessons for Our Own.* New York: Random House, 2020.

Glaude, Eddie S., Jr. *Exodus: Religion, Race, and Nation in Early Nineteenth Century Black America.* Chicago, IL: University of Chicago Press, 2000.

Glaude, Eddie S., Jr. *Democracy in Black: How Race Still Enslaves the American Soul.* New York: Broadway Books, 2016.

Gordon-Reed, Annette, and Peter S. Onuf. *"Most Blessed of the Patriarchs": Thomas Jefferson and the Empire of the Imagination.* New York: W. W. Norton & Company, 2016.

Goza, Joel Edward. *America's Unholy Ghosts: The Racist Roots of Our Faith and Politics.* Eugene, OR: Wipf and Stock Publishers, 2019.

Hayes, Diana L., and Cyprian Davis, eds. *Taking Down Our Harps: Black Catholics in the United States.* New York: Orbis Press, 1998.

Holmes, Barbara A. *Joy Unspeakable: Contemplative Practices of the Black Church.* Minneapolis: Fortress Press, 2017.

Jones, Robert P. *White Too Long: The Legacy of White Supremacy in American Christianity.* New York: Simon & Schuster, 2020.

Kendi, Ibram X. *Stamped from the Beginning: The Definitive History of Racist Ideas in America.* New York: Hachette UK, 2016.

King, Martin Luther, Jr. *Strength to Love.* Minneapolis: Fortress Press, 2010.

King, Martin Luther, Jr. *The Trumpet of Conscience.* New York: Harper & Row, 1967.

156   *Recollecting America's Original Sin*

King, Martin Luther, Jr. *Where Do We Go from Here: Chaos or Community?* King Legacy Series, Vol. 2. Boston, MA: Beacon Press, 2010.

Harvey, Paul. *Bounds of Their Habitation: Race and Religion in American History.* Washington, D.C.: Rowan & Littlefield, 2016.

Harvey, Paul. *Christianity and Race in the American South: A History.* Chicago, IL: University of Chicago Press, 2016.

Lipsitz, George. *The Possessive Investment in Whiteness: How White People Profit from Identity Politics.* Philadelphia, PA: Temple University Press, 2006.

Marty, Martin E. *Pilgrims in Their Own Land: 500 Years of Religion in America.* London: Penguin, 1984.

Massingale, Bryan. *Racial Justice and the Catholic Church.* New York: Orbis Press, 2010.

McGhee, Heather. *The Sum of Us: What Racism Costs Everyone and How We Can Prosper Together.* New York: One World/Ballantine, 2021.

Menakem, Resmaa. *My Grandmother's Hands: Racialized Trauma and the Pathway to Mending Our Hearts and Bodies.* Las Vegas: Central Recovery Press, 2017.

Morton, Marian J. *Cleveland Heights: The Making of an Urban Suburb.* Mount Pleasant, SC: Arcadia Publishing, 2002.

Nepstad, Sharon Erickson. *Catholic Social Activism.* New York: NYU Press, 2019.

Noonan, John. *A Church That Can and Cannot Change.* South Bend, IN: University of Notre Dame Press, 2005.

Painter, Nell Irvin. *The History of White People.* New York: W. W. Norton & Company, 2010.

Phelps, Jamie T., ed. *Black and Catholic: The Challenge and Gift of Black Folk; Contributions of African American Experience and Thought to Catholic Theology.* Milwaukee, WI: Marquette University Press, 1997.

Proenze-Coles, Christina. *American Founders: How People of African Descent Established Freedom in the New World.* Montgomery, AL: NewSouth Books, 2019.

Raboteau, Albert J. *American Prophets: Seven Religious Radicals and Their Struggle for Social and Political Justice.* Princeton, NJ: Princeton University Press, 2016.

Raboteau, Albert J. *Canaan Land: A Religious History of African Americans*. Oxford: Oxford University Press, 1999.

Raboteau, Albert J. *A Fire in the Bones*. Boston, MA: Beacon Press, 1995.

Raboteau, Albert J. *Slave Religion: The "Invisible Institution" in the Antebellum South*. Oxford: Oxford University Press, 2004.

Roediger, David R. *The Wages of Whiteness: Race and the Making of the American Working Class*. London: Verso, 1999.

Roediger, David R. *Working Toward Whiteness: How America's Immigrants Became White; The Strange Journey from Ellis Island to the Suburbs*. New York: Hachette UK, 2006.

Roithmayr, Daria. *Reproducing Racism: How Everyday Choices Lock in White Advantage*. New York: New York University Press, 2014.

Rothstein, Richard. *The Color of Law: A Forgotten History of How Our Government Segregated America*. New York: Liveright Publishing, 2017.

Schneiders, Sandra M. *Beyond Patching: Faith and Feminism in the Catholic Church*. Vol. 1990. Mahwah, NJ: Paulist Press, 2004.

Schneiders, Sandra M. *The Revelatory Text: Interpreting the New Testament as Sacred Scripture*. Collegeville, MN: Liturgical Press, 1999.

Schneiders, Sandra M. *Written That You May Believe: Encountering Jesus in the Fourth Gospel*. Rev. ed. Chestnut Ridge, NY: Crossroad, 2003.

Segura, Olga. *Birth of a Movement: Black Lives Matter and the Catholic Church*. New York: Orbis Press, 2021.

Sernett, Milton C., ed. *African American Religious History: A Documentary Witness*. Durham, NC: Duke University Press, 1999.

Steinhorn, Leonard, and Barbara Diggs-Brown. *By the Color of Our Skin: The Illusion of Integration and the Reality of Race*. New York: Dutton Books, 1999.

Teel, Karen. *Racism and the Image of God*. New York: Palgrave Macmillan, 2010.

Thoreau, Henry. "Walking." *Atlantic Monthly* (June 1862). Reprinted *Atlantic Monthly* (October 2020).

Thurman, Howard. *Deep River and The Negro Spiritual Speaks of Life and Death*. Richmond, IN: Howard Thurman Books, 1975.

Thurman, Howard. *Jesus and the Disinherited*. Boston, MA: Beacon Press, 1996.

Tisby, Jemar. *The Color of Compromise: The Truth about the American Church's Complicity in Racism*. Grand Rapids, MI: Zondervan, 2019.

Turner, Victor. *Dramas, Fields, and Metaphors: Symbolic Action in Human Society*. Ithaca, NY: Cornell University Press, 1974.

United States Conference of Catholic Bishops. Brothers and Sisters to Us: Pastoral Letter on Racism. 1979.

United States Conference of Catholic Bishops. Open Wide Our Hearts: The Enduring Call to Love—A Pastoral Letter Against Racism. 2018.

Wallis, James. *America's Original Sin: Racism, White Privilege, and the Bridge to a New America*. Ada, MI: Brazos Press, 2016.

Wilkerson, Isabel. *Caste: The Origins of Our Discontents*. New York: Random House, 2020.

Wilkerson, Isabel. *The Warmth of Other Suns: The Epic Story of America's Great Migration*. New York: Random House, 2010.

Yancy, George, ed. *Christology and Whiteness: What Would Jesus Do?* Oxfordshire: Routledge, 2012.